Just Say It!

Just Say It!

True Stories about
Witnessing Opportunities

Nellie Pickard

Foreword by George Sweeting

BAKER BOOK HOUSE
Grand Rapids, Michigan 49516

*To my children, **Karen, Tim,** and **Greta**—
and to their God-given mates,
David, Jan, and **Michael.***

*All of you have enriched my life. Your
love for Christ is not in word only
but in your actions.
Thanks for being such caring people.*

Contents

Foreword

Nellie Pickard's book *Just Say It!* is a choice collection of down-to-earth witnessing conversations. Step by step, in an easy-to-read style, Nellie shares suggestions for witnessing to others. This book will bolster your confidence and reduce your fears. I really like Nellie's relaxed, natural approach.

George Sweeting
Moody Bible Institute

Introduction

I'm often told, "I can't witness like you, Nellie." "You're not supposed to witness like I do," I say. "You use the opportunities God gives *you*. God will prepare suitable circumstances just for you. Just say it!"

For the believer, witnessing is neither optional nor an activity to be regarded lightly. Jesus didn't suggest, "Now that I've:

Paid the ultimate price for your redemption,

Died on the cross for your sins,

Taken your guilt on myself,

Given you peace and joy,

And an inheritance and heaven besides—

Maybe you ought to tell someone about it." No, witnessing is a command of the Lord, a joyous responsibility.

Acts 1:8 tells us, "You will receive power when the Holy Spirit comes on you; and you will be my witnesses in Jerusalem, and in all Judea and Samaria, and to the ends of the earth." That means believers will have the strength and ability to witness all over the place—to neighbors and co-workers, in the supermarket or on the tennis court—wherever and whenever the opportunity presents itself.

If you are in the family of God and desire to obey his commands, the secret is to be available to the Lord always. It's a simple matter of stepping out in faith. Just say it!

My friend Irene Franklin told my husband an interesting story:

> I gave a copy of Nellie's book to one of my friends at church. When she finished, her husband, who works for the airlines, picked it up, read it, and commented, "She makes it sound so easy. It seems the author is saying that all you have to do is be available."
>
> "Why don't you tell the Lord you want to be available to him for witnessing," his wife suggested.
>
> "Well, okay," he said, and that was his prayer that night.
>
> When the man came home from work the following evening, he said to his wife, "I can't believe what happened today! A fellow at work came to me and said, 'I've been reading the Bible lately and there are a lot of things I don't understand. I wonder if you would mind explaining some of the verses to me.'
>
> "I told the Lord last night I wanted to be available to him, but I didn't think it would happen so soon!"

Obviously this man already had a witness by his lifestyle, or his co-worker would not have asked him to interpret some biblical passages. An exemplary lifestyle, however, is not enough. To win others to Christ, we need to talk Scripture. Then God's Word does the convicting.

When I talked to Irene on the phone this morning, she said, "My friend told me last Sunday, 'Opportunities for witnessing have exploded ever since I became available to the Lord. And now my husband, too, is excited about sharing his faith.'"

If you mean business about serving the Lord and sharing his gospel, God will give you many opportunities to be a witness for him. You don't need to devise some complicated plan, or spontaneously grab everyone you meet, if you want to tell people the Good News. Instead, just mean it when you say, "Lord, I'm available. Send me." He'll do his part by showing you when and to whom you should "just say it."

This book will include some of my own witnessing experiences and those of my friends. I hope it will point out that we all need to share our faith and encourage each other in as many ways as possible. Perhaps partly because I have written two previous books on witnessing, people seem to feel secure in relating their experiences to me. They know I am interested and am delighted to hear them. I am especially happy when someone says, "Your books have encouraged me to speak out for the Lord."

Every believer has been challenged by the Great Commission to "go and make disciples of all nations" (Matt. 28:19). If we truly love God and want to serve him, our faith in his saving message of grace must not remain a secret. So we Just Say It!—with joy and gratitude in our hearts.

[Jesus said:] "A new command I give you: Love one another. As I have loved you, so you must love one another. By this all men will know that you are my disciples, if you love one another."

[John 13:34–35]

1

The Newcomers

M y name's Mary Martin," the voice on the phone said. "I'm not sure you remember me. You autographed my book when I attended the 'Walk through the Bible' at your church. At the time, I told you that my children attend your Christian school but I'm a member of a Presbyterian church."

"It's been some time ago, but I think I do remember talking to you," I answered.

"I have a new friend who is attending our church," Mary said. "She's from New York and doesn't know many people in this area. She seems drawn to the people in our congregation, yet I don't believe she understands the Scriptures and God's way of salvation. After reading your book, I thought you might be of help to her. Would you be willing to have lunch with us?"

"Sure! I'm tied up until after the holidays but I'm available after the first of the year." So we arranged a meeting for January 8 at Mary's house.

Mary lived about five miles from my home. The garage door was open when I arrived, making it convenient to enter through the back door and so avoid the heavy drifts of snow.

"Welcome to my home," Mary said as she ushered me into the kitchen. "Nellie, meet Jennifer." I turned to see a young woman bent over as she tried to put on her boots.

"I'm sorry," she said, "I meant to have these on before you arrived. I've been in my stocking feet all morning."

"Jennifer's been here all morning helping me," Mary explained. "In fact, she made the lunch. She's a good cook."

I peeked over at the counter and noticed three plates, on each of which was chicken salad in a hollowed-out tomato, with carrot and raisin salad alongside.

Jennifer finally got her boots on and stood up. She looked to be in her early thirties and was quite pretty. *Different, but cute,* I remember thinking. Under her eyebrows was deep pink eye shadow. Below that was blue shadow and lots of mascara on her lashes. She wore one dangling earring. Though a large cross hung around her neck, her blouse was unbuttoned to the waist. I pretended not to notice. It was as if she was trying to make a statement, perhaps testing her new friends to see if they would accept her as she was.

"Come here, so I can give my new friend a hug," I said. Jennifer hugged me back real hard. The ice was broken.

I asked Jennifer how she liked Michigan.

"I hate it," she said. "We hadn't lived here long when someone shot bullet holes through the window of our home. When we called the police they told us they'd been having trouble with kids shooting at houses as they drove by."

"That certainly wasn't a very good reception to our fair state. I hope you meet some nicer people," I said sympathetically.

"Oh, I have," she said. "The people at church are great. I've never experienced such love anywhere."

"Do you have children?" I asked.

"No, I don't. I'm a nurse and I worked in a children's psychiatric ward when I lived in New York. I loved the children but I'm not sure I want any of my own."

At that point Jennifer excused herself. "I need a cigarette," she explained as she put on a beautiful fur coat and went outside. *A person of contrasts*, I thought.

When she returned I asked, "As a nurse, do you agree that smoking contributes to the incidence of cancer?" (It concerned me that her voice sounded husky.)

"Absolutely! But I like to smoke," she said nonchalantly.

"Well, Jennifer, the Bible says, 'A man reaps what he sows' [Gal. 6:7b]. If you develop cancer from your smoking, you won't blame God, will you?"

"No, I'll take the blame. It will be my own fault. But I've got endometriosis and I didn't do anything to deserve *that*. If God loves me, why did he let this happen?"

"God created everything perfect in the beginning," I said, "but Man's sin brought consequences. Sickness and death are some of the troubles we now face as a result of our disobedience."

Mary put the food on the table and invited us to sit down.

"Nellie, before we give thanks for the food," said our hostess, "I want you to know I've told Jennifer all about you. She'd like to discuss some of her viewpoints concerning God, the Bible, and life in general. I told her I thought you'd be willing to listen and maybe answer some of her questions."

Jennifer was outgoing and had no problem expressing herself. "When I came here from New York," she said, "I didn't know a soul. My husband and I were lonesome. I left the church I was raised in because I was disillusioned, but when we arrived in this area, I looked in the newspapers to find a church. I had visited a Presbyterian church in New Jersey and liked it, so I decided I'd try one here. I called one near our home and was surprised when the minister answered. He was very cordial and we chatted for about twenty minutes. He told me the time of the service and my husband and I attended the next Sunday. When I arrived, though I knew immediately that I was not like those people, their friendliness amazed me."

At this point Mary laughed and said, "Well, I'll admit your appearance was—well, different."

"I suppose you're right. But one of the women came over after the service and introduced herself. 'I'm Sandy,' she said. 'I see you're new. I'd like to take you out to lunch next week.' I looked at her and thought, *We're not one bit alike. No way is she going to like me. I'd better tell her a few things about myself.* So I said, 'Well, you need to know that I smoke, I drink, I curse, and I like sex.' Sandy didn't even blink before she asked what day was convenient for me.

"She's been my friend ever since. I can't get over the

love these people show me. It amazes me that they don't judge me at all. And I love them, too. I don't agree with everything they say or teach, but they don't mind if I ask questions, even when I say, 'Prove it!'

"One night the fellow in charge prayed for me," Jennifer went on. "He actually asked God to bless me for making them look up the answers to the questions I asked. No one has ever asked God to bless me. It was incredible. But they talk about submission to God at that church, and I'm never going to submit to anyone," she said firmly. "My husband and I are liberated. We don't believe in submission." She waited for me to respond.

I began by telling her that my first book—*What Do You Say When?*　was dedicated to Paul, my husband. Then I said, "His life verse is Ephesians 5:25: 'Husbands, love your wives, just as Christ loved the church and gave himself up for her.' Do you think I'd have any problem submitting to someone who loved me that much?"

"That same chapter tells us that partners in a marriage are to submit *to each other* for their mutual benefit. It's not talking about lording it over each other. A corporation has a president. A shop or store has a manager. Someone has to be in charge or else there would be chaos. I've committed my life to Jesus Christ," I explained. "It's the best decision I've ever made. I've never regretted it. In submitting to him, I'm safe and free to do what is right—because I know God loves me."

Jennifer changed that subject and commented, "I don't think God is fair. I don't see why he doesn't let Buddhists, Muslims, and people of other faiths into heaven. If he was really a God of love, he'd do that."

"Sounds like you want to make the rules, Jennifer. Maybe you'd like to be God," I said with a smile.

"Of course not, but it still doesn't seem fair," she answered.

My answer was: "Jesus said, 'I am the way and the truth and the life. No one comes to the Father except through me' [John 14:6]. If you could get to heaven any other way, his death on the cross would have been a total waste. There would have been no need for him to die.

"Do you realize," I went on, "that Jesus, who was sinless, actually paid the penalty for our sins. He opted to be our substitute. *We* deserved to die on the cross, but because of God's great love for us, he was willing to take our place."

"What happens to people who don't believe in Christ?" Jennifer asked.

I said, "The Bible tells us they will be cast into outer darkness. God says, 'You shall have no other gods before me' [Exod. 20:3]."

I looked at my watch and realized it was getting late. "I'm going to have to leave, Jennifer. But, before I go, would you like to read a booklet that gives the basics of the Bible? It's helped a lot of people understand God's requirements for salvation."

The booklet I planned to give Jennifer was *The Four Spiritual Laws,* which is distributed by Campus Crusade for Christ. I like to use it because it forces people to face their spiritual condition. The booklet begins with "God loves you and has a wonderful plan for your life."

We went into the den and sat down. I began reading aloud about God's love in sending his Son to die for our sins. I explained to Jennifer that the only way we can approach our holy God is through Jesus Christ. "That's why it's so important that we admit or confess that we're sinners and accept him as our Savior. In fact, the greatest sin you can commit is not murder, but rejecting

Jesus Christ. Jennifer, where do you think Jesus is in relation to you right now?"

"I think he's in my life—a little." She seemed hesitant.

"Jesus can't be in your life 'a little.' He's either in or he's not. You remind me of a woman in my Bible class," I said. "She claimed Jesus was out on the porch. She hadn't invited him inside. I told her that wasn't very polite. She wouldn't keep a friend standing at her closed front door. She'd invite that friend into her home.

"This is what Jesus says in Revelation 3:20: 'Here I am! I stand at the door and knock. If anyone hears my voice and opens the door, I will come in and eat with him, and he with me.' He's knocking at *your* door, Jennifer. What are you going to do about it?"

She started to cry. "I want to invite him in. I want him to be my Savior."

After praying through her tears, Jennifer asked Jesus to be Lord of her life.

"You know, Jennifer, an hour ago you said, 'I'm *never* going to submit to anyone. I'm a liberated woman.' Now you belong to the family of God. You belong to the King of kings. You're special in his sight. Would you like to thank him? I'll pray first."

When I finished praying, she began, "Hi, Lord, this is me, you know, Jennifer."

My heart melted as she thanked the Lord for all that had happened that day and ended with: "I believe that with Jesus I'm going to make it. In fact, I won't give up, because I *know* I can make it," she repeated.

"When I see you again," she said to me, "I would like to tell you why I was so adamant about not submitting to anyone. I really want to tell you about myself."

As I left, I reminded Jennifer that she was a child of the King, which made her special.

I've talked to Jennifer a few times since that day. On one occasion she told me that when the news of the war with Iraq was announced, she was greatly disturbed and frightened. She kept her ears glued to the television set all day. When evening came she said to her husband, "I can't listen another minute. Please give me the book."

"What book?" he asked.

"You know, *the* book—the good book—the Bible," Jennifer said. "I don't know what part I'll read, but God will show me," she had insisted.

Later she commented to me:

> I turned to the Psalms and read the first ten chapters. It was so exciting. It tells what's going to happen to the nations that turn against the Lord. But if we trust God, he will bless us. Because he's in control, I don't have anything to be afraid of. I now go to sleep with my Bible next to my pillow. I wake up often in the middle of the night. I used to read a novel at such times, but now I read my Bible and it comforts me.

"I'm anxious for you to meet my husband," Jennifer then added. "Richard is the greatest—so good and kind. You'll just love him."

"We'll plan to get together soon," I promised.

I met Richard sooner than either of us had expected.

Mary called the following Thursday afternoon. "I know it's late to be calling," she said. "But we just learned it's Jennifer's birthday. We've arranged for Richard to bring her to the pizza place. Several families from the church want to surprise her. It would mean a lot to her if you and your husband could come."

"Oh, I'm sorry, but I'm supposed to be at a writers' group meeting."

"It would mean so much to Jennifer if you could come," Mary urged.

"Well, I guess she is my top priority these days," I said. "I'll cancel my engagement."

It was interesting to watch Jennifer's face when she entered the restaurant. She saw many familiar faces, both children and adults. All of them were her friends. She was speechless when they shouted, "Surprise!"

Jennifer cried, laughed, stammered, and stuttered. Then she saw me. "I just can't believe it," she went on and on. I thought she would never settle down.

"Richard, you've got to meet Nellie." Jennifer brought her husband over and introduced us. I also introduced them to Paul.

Richard was tall and pleasant-looking and seemed to have a gentleness about him. I liked him immediately. It was evident that he and Jennifer loved each other very much. He was as pleased as Jennifer when she was presented with a gift certificate to the local Christian bookstore.

"Ours is a Presbyterian church, and you belong to a Baptist church," Jennifer said to me later in the evening. "What's the difference?"

"There are a few differences, but the basics are the same. Your pastor's children and Mary's children attend our Christian school. We all get along quite well," I said.

"I'd like to visit your church with Richard," she replied.

It took about three weeks before our schedules would allow us to get together. Paul and I met the young couple in the foyer of our church. Our sanctuary is large and was a bit overwhelming to them, since the church they were attending was new and rather small. The group met in a school building, but finer people would be hard to find. They are known throughout the community by their love.

At our church, Jennifer and Richard entered right into the singing. When the opening music was finished, we were asked to greet the people near us. I introduced the couple to several people, and later they got a chance to meet Pastor Crowley.

Seven people were baptized that night. I knew that neither Jennifer nor Richard had ever witnessed adult baptism, but they seemed to enjoy the service.

When the service was over, they came home with us for a bite to eat and we had a chance to talk.

"Tell me about baptism. I was baptized as a baby. Does that count?" Jennifer asked.

I said, "Tonight you witnessed believers' baptism. Though it doesn't save a person, it is an outward demonstration of what has happened to that person on the inside. It tells the world that you identify with Jesus' death, burial, and resurrection.

"In many churches, parents bring their babies to be baptized as a dedication to the Lord, promising to raise their children in the nurture and admonition of God. I've heard others say that baptism saved them, but Scripture doesn't teach that. In order to be saved, a person has to confess that he or she has sinned against holy God. Then they must receive Jesus Christ as their personal Savior."

I pointed out that all those who were baptized that night gave their testimony about how they came to Christ. Some told of their rebellion against God at one point in their life. Others told of attending church but never understanding what it meant to have a personal relationship with Jesus Christ.

"Richard," I said, "I don't know you well, but you seem to be such a kind person, and that's how the pastor of the church you're attending described you. But in Romans 3:22–23 the Bible says, 'This righteousness from God comes through faith in Jesus Christ. . . . For all have sinned and fall short of the glory of God.' Where do you stand in the light of those verses?"

"Well, I've not had the struggles Jennifer has had throughout her life. I don't think I've rebelled against God."

"I believe you," I said. "But that doesn't make you right before God. Why don't we go step-by-step through the little booklet I gave Jennifer? That way you can be sure where you stand with the Lord. You don't want to take anything for granted."

Richard seemed to understand that Jesus Christ died on the cross for our sins. But then I asked him, "Where is Christ in relation to you? Is he on the throne of your life or are you pretty much in control of your life?"

He hesitated to ponder that question, but finally answered, "I wish I could say that he was running my life. I think I'm pretty much in control of things, but. . . ." Then he looked at me and said, "I'd like *Jesus* to take control. I really would."

It was a beautiful moment. Jennifer sat on the floor next to Richard's chair. She touched his arm as he prayed and asked Jesus Christ to be Lord of his life. We all rejoiced together. I thanked the Lord for Richard's commitment. Then he prayed again, thanking the Lord for making salvation plain to him. It was clear that for the first time he understood what it was all about.

"Now we're really together," Jennifer said with tears in her eyes.

Postscript

Events such as these allow me to see the power of the Holy Spirit at work. Because there is no greater joy than to be a part of God's work, I am grateful to be God's instrument.

All believers need other Christians to help them grow in their faith. Every day, Mary and Jennifer read a chapter in the Bible together and pray. What a boost for any new believer! Richard attends Bible study on Saturdays with the men from his church. Ralph Rebandt, their pastor, is a tremendous help and encouragement to these young people. My verse for Jennifer and Richard is Philippians 1:6: "Being confident of this, that he who began a good work in you will carry it on to completion until the day of Christ Jesus."

Recently Jennifer told me about the circumstances in her past that made the very idea of submitting to the Lord—or anyone—so painful. "I was a victim of incest," she said. "My father, a psychiatrist, took advantage of me until I was eleven years old. The word *submission* had always brought fear to my heart. But now I know that submitting to Jesus Christ is liberating. It brings real freedom.

"I also want you to know that I no longer hate my father. I have only pity for him. O, yes, I had anger and rage to work through, but I don't hate him anymore. He was a tormented man. He's dead now, I've forgiven him and I wish I could have helped him. My desire now is to help other victims of abuse. Now I know that God can help them get through their pain, just as he helped me."

Can Presbyterians and Baptists work together for the Lord? You bet!

Do not be overcome by evil, but overcome evil with good.

[Romans 12:21]

2

Not Really So "Different"

I knew it! I knew something would happen sooner or later. How dare that woman!" Dorcas said angrily to her husband. She held the curtain aside with one hand and the phone with the other.

"What's wrong, honey?" Bob asked. "What are you so upset about?"

"That Iraqi woman next door took our brand-new snow shovel," she told him. "I knew the minute I laid eyes on those people that I wouldn't be able to trust them. They're so different from us."

"Why, only a few weeks ago you had plans to invite our new neighbors to church," Bob said. "The movers hadn't even unloaded their furniture, yet you could hardly wait to meet them."

"Well—that's before I got a good look. Then I discovered they barely speak English. There are people coming and going all day long, speaking what sounds like gibberish. When I realized that even if I wanted to, we wouldn't be able to communicate with each other, I decided to stay as far away as I could. The incident this morning proves what kind of people they are. Besides, with all my responsibilities and busy life, I don't see why I should be required to be neighborly to people with whom I have nothing in common."

"Aren't you being a bit judgmental? Have you forgotten that all our steps are ordered by the Lord? Seems to me I remember you saying that you were going to pray for them," Bob reminded her.

"Yes, I did, but my problem right now is what to do about our snow shovel. Our own porch and sidewalk need attention."

"Wait until she's finished shoveling. If she doesn't bring our shovel back, go over and tell her you need it. That's simple enough," he replied patiently.

Two hours later, Dorcas picked up the phone and called Betty, her best friend, and told her the story. "That woman didn't bring our shovel back. Bob says I should go to get it before I leave for work. What shall I do?"

"Ring her doorbell," Betty said, "and when she comes to the door, be firm. Let her know you mean business. I'll hang up right now and pray that you will do the right thing."

Dorcas dressed for work, got in her car, and angrily backed it into the neighbors' driveway. (She thought she might need a quick getaway.) When she walked up the steps to the porch, she saw her shovel covered with a piece of plastic. She put one hand on the shovel and the other on the doorbell. Before she could push the button, the door opened and there stood her neighbor.

"I see you borrowed my shovel," Dorcas said coldly. "I'll be taking it back now." She turned and walked toward her car. To her surprise the woman called out in broken English.

"No, no—I bring back later. I just take—bring back later."

"No, I'll take it *now*," Dorcas insisted. She took the shovel home and left for work. Her day was ruined. The thought of that incident infuriated her. Consumed with bitterness and anger, she found it hard to concentrate on her work.

"The nerve of that woman," she told her co-workers. "I can't believe she'd do such a thing. She obviously thinks, *What's theirs is mine.*"

As Dorcas was driving home from work, she thought, *I've got to get rid of this bitter feeling and stop thinking about my neighbor. I should be concentrating on my message for the retreat this weekend.* "Let's see: 'Blessed are the merciful,'" she repeated out loud. That verse, Matthew 5:7, was her assigned topic for the mother-and-daughter retreat. "'Blessed are the merciful, for they will be shown mercy.'" *Blessed are the merciful—blessed are the merciful*—those words rang through her mind over and over again until she could think of nothing else. Finally Dorcas said, "Okay, Lord, I hear what you're saying. I'll do it. I'll be merciful."

The Spirit of God impressed on Dorcas's mind and heart that she should buy her neighbors a new snow shovel. She knew she had to be obedient to God's promptings, so she stopped at the hardware store and purchased one. She put a big red bow on the shovel, added a friendly note, and placed it on her neighbors' porch. Suddenly Dorcas was exhilarated and began to feel good about herself. *If I don't practice what I preach,* she thought, *I am a hypocrite. Blessed are the merciful. And I can be merciful—I want to be merciful.* Love replaced the bitterness in her heart.

The next day, as Dorcas went about packing her suitcase for the retreat, she was inexplicably reminded of her rebellious teenage years. *But God in his mercy saved me. In turn, I have to be merciful to my neighbors,* she thought.

Dorcas picked up her luggage, ready to leave, when the doorbell rang. There stood her new neighbor, holding a baked specialty from her own country, hot from the oven and smelling delicious.

"You give shovel me? Tank you much—me all lone—two children—me no shovel—me no car—me no gets K-Marts."

"It's a gift from God," Dorcas said.

"Tank you—My name Nazah. Tank you much," the woman said with a shy smile and turned to leave.

Dorcas closed the door and began to cry. "Thank you, Lord for not letting me get away with being unneighborly. Now I'm free before you to speak to others."

Because of that incident, Dorcas started having coffee with her neighbor on a regular basis. It has been a time of getting acquainted and learning about each other's ways and customs. Little by little, Dorcas is sharing with Nazah her faith and trust in Jesus Christ.

Nazah allowed her two small children to attend Vacation Bible School that summer. Dorcas experienced unmeasurable joy when she heard the tiny six-year-old girl singing as she was riding her bicycle up and down the street: "Jesus loves me, this I know, for the Bible tells me so." It was one of the songs the child had learned during those few weeks!

Dorcas had related this story to me some time ago, and I was eager to hear if there were any new developments. I recently saw her after church and asked, "How are you getting along with your new neighbor?"

"Got a few minutes?" she asked as she smiled broadly. I sat down and listened as she continued her story.

"Even though Nazah is not attending church with us, she allows her children to attend Sunday school. It's a beginning. And I know I've been able to help her feel at home here. Bob and I had decided some time ago to fix up our house and move to a different location. But when Nazah saw our 'For Sale' sign she said, 'I pray God you no move. You move—I move—next door your house.'

"You know, Nellie," Dorcas continued, "it's not easy to live next door to someone from another culture. Our standards and way of life are so different. But God placed Nazah and her children there. He is sovereign, and he makes no mistakes.

"I took Nazah out for lunch last week. She is very appreciative, and I'm gradually getting to know her better. Bob and I are grateful that she trusts us enough to let her children come to Sunday school. I pray that God will give me wisdom as I spend time with her. Perhaps Nazah, too, will soon understand how much God loves her."

I thought I had finished writing this story but yesterday Dorcas came to me at church and said excitedly, "This morning, on the way to Sunday school, Magdee, Nazah's nine-year-old son, told us he had received Jesus Christ as his Savior."

"How did that come about?" I asked.

"The Spirit of God opened his heart as he read a little

booklet Bob had given him. It talked about God's love in sending Jesus Christ to die for our sins. 'I read it over and over,' Magdee said, 'and then I checked it out to see if it was the same as the Bible you gave me. Everything was the same, so I prayed and asked Jesus to come into my heart and be my Savior. I signed my name after the prayer—see!'

"We were so amazed that we questioned him over and over again to see if he understood. Finally he looked at us as if to say, 'Don't you believe me?' Bob turned to him and said, 'We believe you.'

"We knew that Magdee's mother had constantly threatened him with, 'You be good, or God gonna get you.' Then she would shake her finger at him. But when Magdee read about God's love, his heart responded. He needed to know that although God judges, he also forgives and loves us with an everlasting love. I hope Nazah will soon understand that, too."

Postscript

Only God knows the ending of this story, but the apostle Paul has said, "And the peace of God, which transcends all understanding, will guard your hearts and minds in Christ Jesus" (Phil. 4:7). It is required of a servant to be faithful, but only God can give the increase. Even believers have a tendency to stick up for our rights. We are angry when we discover someone has taken advantage of us. *I'm not going to let my neighbor get away with stealing my shovel,* Dorcas thought, until the Holy Spirit reminded her of the very Scripture she was to talk about at the retreat. Because Dorcas responded to God's promptings to be merciful, she was given a creative alternative.

[Jesus said:] "If someone forces you to go one mile, go with him two miles. Give to the one who asks you, and do not turn away from the one who wants to borrow from you." [Matt. 5:41–42]

Live in harmony with one another. Do not be proud. . . . If it is possible, as far as it depends on you, live at peace with everyone. [Rom. 12:16, 18]

*Give thanks in all circumstances, for this is
God's will for you in Christ Jesus.*

[1 Thessalonians 5:18]

3

Frustration or Opportunity?

"O h, no! Not again," I groaned to my husband. "We just had the car fixed last week. Here we are at the top of Lewiston Bridge, almost in the good old U.S.A., and the car stops. Just look at the line-up behind us and in front of us. What in the world can we do? We'll never get out of here!"

"Well, Nellie, be thankful we got this far," Paul said. "If our car had stopped on the way up, we'd be stuck here all day. You steer and I'll push the car downhill. Be sure to put on the brakes when you get close to the car in front of you."

You might guess that Paul doesn't get upset easily! He just does what he has to do. As he started to push the car, I sent up an SOS to my heavenly Father. "How are you going to get us out of this one?" I prayed. Then I saw a man get out of his car and come toward us. "Let me help you, pal," he said to my husband. "My wife will drive our car. I'll catch up with her at the bottom of the hill."

"I really appreciate your help," Paul said.

"Are you out of gas?" the man asked.

"No, I've plenty of gas. I don't know what's wrong. I had it in for repairs a couple of days ago. I thought everything was in good running order. But if I get it past customs into the States, I can call AAA and get help."

We paid our toll and looked for a place to park, but the spaces were all taken. Then I heard the stranger call his wife, "Here we are, honey."

"I've been waiting for you," she said. "I saved a place so they can park their car. Be ready to push it in after I back out."

My, such wonderful people, I thought. *What can we do to show our appreciation? I know they won't accept money.*

After I parked the car, I got out and thanked both of them. "You are so kind. You were an answer to my prayer," I said. "I'd like to give you a copy of my book *What Do You Say When?* It's about sharing my faith in Jesus Christ. Do you have a church background?" I asked.

"Yes, we belong to the Anglican Church," the man answered.

"I hope my book will encourage you in the faith," I said. "And thank you again for your kindness."

Paul went to call AAA. Though he tried several times, he couldn't get through. "What's the problem?" I asked.

"The lines are busy. It's been a half hour since I made the first call."

We had hoped to get to the Connecticut home of our daughter Greta and her husband, Michael Blanchard, before dark, but now that seemed impossible. Then I thought of God's words in Psalms: "Call upon me in the day of trouble; I will deliver you, and you will honor me" (Ps. 50:15).

"We're in trouble, Lord," I prayed. "We ask you to deliver us. We trust you and want to honor you in all things."

I took a walk while Paul was figuring out our next step. When I heard the beep of a horn, I turned around, and saw him in the driver's seat. "Come on," he said. "The car seems to be okay."

"Thank you, Lord," I breathed. Paul said, "Amen."

We drove all day without any more trouble. Because we had lost so much time at the bridge, we had to drive into the evening hours. At times it seemed as though we were alone in a wilderness, driving up and down hills and around steep curves. *I sure hope we don't get stuck on one of these roads,* I thought. Then I remembered that God had provided help before. Now I must continue to trust him.

With grateful hearts we arrived safe and sound and greeted Greta and Michael with warm hugs. After we unloaded the car, Paul decided to move it to give Michael more room for his vehicle. Our car wouldn't start! But we still went to sleep that night with the sense of God's protection.

We had to have the car fixed twice while in Connecticut. One time, while we were waiting at the repair shop, a tall blonde young man came into the office to pay his bill. Since we both had to wait, we got into a conversation. At one point I said, "I'm curious. I'm wondering why you wear an earring. Would you mind telling me?"

"Oh, that," he said as he touched his ear. "I usually forget I have it on. That's a leftover from my rebellious years when I went to college in California. I'm a responsible person now."

"You mean you've made things right with the people you rebelled against?"

"Well, yeah. It was mostly my parents. But things are all right now," he said pleasantly.

"What about God?" I asked. "Have you made things right with him?"

"I'm not much for religion. When I was a kid, my parents made me go to Unity, but I didn't believe those teachings. I really don't know what the truth is."

"I can understand that," I smiled, "but you ought to start reading the Bible. That's where you'll find truth. By the way, would you be interested in taking this booklet to read? It covers the basics of what the Bible teaches. I've shared it with many people."

"I'd like that. I'm always looking for something to read when I go on business trips and have to wait for a customer. Well, looks like my car is ready. I'm glad we talked. Thanks again for the booklet." He shook my hand and left.

A few minutes later, Paul walked in and said, "I think they've found the trouble. The car should be okay for a while."

A few days later, we went to visit our daughter Karen and her husband, David Green, in Massachusetts. That weekend I was scheduled to speak at a women's retreat in Waldoburo, Maine. Since we arrived at both places without incident, we returned to the Greens and began to relax about the car.

Whenever we visit, Karen usually has a list of things for Paul to fix. (Having a dad who is an engineer comes in handy at times.) "Here's my list," she said. "It doesn't matter which you pick. I'll be grateful for anything you do."

Because we knew the kitchen was important to Karen, we decided to tackle some remodeling there first. All of us would pitch in. Paul did most of the work, but David took a day off from his job and was a big help. It was great to see Paul and our son-in-law working so well together and actually making it seem like fun.

At one point Karen asked, "Mom, do you want to take me to the hardware store? I'd like to pick out some new pulls for the drawers. Dad and David are going to fetch the countertops, so you'll have to drive."

"No problem," I said. "The car seems to be running fine. Let's go."

Driving in the Boston area is treacherous, especially on Route 128. I was so glad to park the car at the store that I heaved a sigh of relief.

We found just the right pulls, which made Karen happy. This would put the finishing touches on the kitchen, so we were both excited as we headed for the car. I turned the key in the ignition, but nothing happened. "Oh, no! Not again"—the same words I had uttered just two weeks before.

"Well," I said, "we know God's in control of our lives. Let's pray." We both prayed for wisdom—and patience.

"Karen, do you know we've had this car fixed five times in the past two weeks? Yet the Lord protected us in every situation. What if the car had stopped on Route 128? I shudder to think about it. I don't know what God wants to teach us, but we'll trust him and thank him."

We called home and Paul and David came to help us. They called a car dealer. Since it was Friday afternoon, we didn't know what kind of service we would get. The dealer said, "Sorry, we can't help you until Tuesday. We're busy today, we don't work on Saturday and Sunday, and Monday is Columbus Day. You'll have to wait until Tuesday."

On Tuesday I was supposed to be back in Michigan to speak! *Remember,* I told myself, *God's in control. Trust him.*

Paul then called another dealer, who said, "We'll send a mechanic right out. We would rather not tow the car if possible. It may disturb the part that needs fixing. He'll be there in about twenty minutes."

It wasn't long before the young mechanic drove up and parked right next to our car. He made a few tests, checked under the hood, and then said, "Yep, I think I've spotted the problem. I'll make a temporary adjustment so the car will run. Then you follow me." In short order the car was running again. We followed the mechanic to the dealer, who suggested we walk over to the nearby mall and have lunch. "By the time you're through, the car will be just about ready." We were greatly relieved.

We actually relaxed enough to enjoy our lunch. When we went back to pick up our car, five other people were in the dealer's waiting room. One of the men wanted to know what had happened to our car. Paul told him our story, starting from the Lewiston Bridge.

Then I added, "I sure don't enjoy driving on Route 128. I'm glad the car didn't stop in the middle of traffic."

"You could have been killed," the man said dramatically (as if I didn't know!).

"That's right. But if I *had* been killed, I know I would go to be with the Lord."

"How do you know you'd be with the Lord? How do you really know?" the man challenged me.

"First of all," I said, "you need to know that I don't expect to go to heaven because I'm a good person. Heaven is not a reward for any good things I might have done. The Bible says that 'all have sinned and fall short of the glory of God' [Rom. 3:23]. We can never reach God's standards. He demands perfection."

"Sounds like we're in big trouble," he said.

"We would be, if it weren't for Jesus Christ. Only *he* is perfect. He died on the cross for our sins and is the mediator between God and man. If we confess to God that we are sinners and receive Jesus Christ as our Savior, he will accept us. John 3:16 says, 'For God so loved the world that he gave his one and only Son, that whoever believes in him shall not perish but have eternal life.' On the basis of my confession of faith in Jesus Christ, I know I'm going to heaven. I have eternal life. I received that the moment I believed. . . ."

"Say, do you want to hear a good joke?" the man's wife interrupted.

She had a wicked gleam in her eye, so I said, "Not really."

"Oh, but this is a good one." She proceeded to tell an off-color story. Her husband touched her gently and said, "Please, don't do that."

She ignored him and continued dominating the conversation. "I want you to know that many times people mistake me for Helen Hayes. And I'm considered the life of the party. You see, I believe in having fun."

"Please don't talk like that," her husband said quietly. After the rest of the people in the room showed distaste by the expression on their faces, the woman kept quiet for a while.

"I'm a retired newspaper reporter," her husband said. "I've read many books and enjoy reading, but there are two writings I have difficulty understanding: Shakespeare's works and the Bible."

"I don't know much about Shakespeare, but I can tell you why you don't understand the Bible," I replied. "You have to read it with eyes of faith."

"How do you get faith?" he asked.

"The Bible says in Romans 10:17: 'Faith comes from hearing the message, and the message is heard through the word of Christ.' So if you want faith, you have to read the Bible and believe what you read."

"I've scanned it but where should I start?" he wanted to know.

"I suggest you start in the Book of John. It's a good place to get acquainted with Jesus Christ. Perhaps you could read it to your wife as well."

"Yes, we can read it together," he said as he took his wife's hand. She laughed nervously and said, "Yeah, that will be okay."

A woman sitting across the room from us joined in the conversation. "My son used to be very hot-tempered and rebellious. But ever since he's gotten this Christianity bit, he's changed. I can't get over it. Someone hit his car the other day. Once I would have expected him to be madder than a wet hen, but he just took everything calmly. I tell you he's a different person now."

I nodded and said, "Well, that's what happens when a person receives Christ. It's a transformed life."

The woman sitting next to me whispered, "I'm glad

you spoke to those people. As soon as my car is ready, I'll be on my way to a Bible study class." She showed me her workbook. They were studying Exodus. "This has been an interesting experience," she added.

"Pickard, please go to the cashier. Your car's ready," the voice over the loudspeaker broke in.

Postscript

I have reflected much on the events of that day and the two preceding weeks. I can't help thinking that what could have been a series of frustrations turned out to be an ongoing opportunity to witness for the Lord.

Adversity can teach us many lessons. We learn, first of all, that there is pain in frustration but joy in the opportunity it often presents. Most of us must learn the hard way, but believers have a choice. We can complain and grumble about the irksome situations in which we find ourselves. Or we can be "always giving thanks to God the Father for everything, in the name of our Lord Jesus Christ" (Eph. 5:20). Whatever the circumstance, there is always a way to do God's will with joy and thanksgiving.

Some of the Pharisees in the crowd said to Jesus, "Teacher, rebuke your disciples!"

"I tell you," he replied, "if they keep quiet, the stones will cry out."

[Luke 19:39–40]

4

Pain with a Purpose

"Do you realize we've been driving for twelve hours?" I commented to my husband. "I think we'd better stop at the next town. I'm exhausted."

"I'm ready to call it quits, too," Paul said. "I've got a strange pain in my back. It's probably from sitting in the same position for so long."

It had been a beautiful day. We had stopped in Dayton, Ohio, to visit our friend Kenny Wyckoff, something we often did on our way to Florida. Her husband had gone home to be with the Lord a few years ago, so these stopovers were special to us.

"Tifton, Georgia, is just a few miles down the road," Paul said. "It will be a good place to stop."

We found a take-out restaurant and bought some food to eat in our motel room. A few hours later, Paul said, "I'm not sure the pain in my back is from driving. It's getting worse and spreading from my back to my stomach. Maybe a good hot bath will help."

Though he soaked in the tub for about half an hour, it didn't seem to help. I could see Paul was in pain, but he had never been seriously ill, so I didn't think too much about it.

We read, watched the news on TV, and tried to relax before we retired for the evening. Around midnight Paul sat up in bed and groaned, "Nellie, something is definitely wrong. This is no ordinary pain. I'd better get to a hospital right away."

I was frightened. Here we were in a motel, hundreds of miles from home and friends. What was I to do?

"Lord, help us," I prayed. Then I called the motel desk and asked for directions to the nearest hospital.

"It's seven miles down the highway with a few turns here and there. Stop at the desk and I'll sketch out a map," said the night clerk.

I was tense as we drove away from the motel. By this time, Paul was writhing in pain, doubled over and moaning. I had never seen him like this. *Is it a heart attack?* I wondered. "Oh, Lord, help us to find the way quickly," I prayed fervently.

We followed the directions carefully and found the hospital without any problem. The "Emergency" sign was in plain view, which was quite a relief.

The attendants could see Paul's condition was serious. "We'll take care of your husband," one of the men said. "You go to the desk and have him registered." When they took Paul through the double doors, a horrible thought ran through my mind: *I wonder if I'll ever see him alive again.*

I went to the desk and gave the registrar the information she requested.

"What is your religious preference?" she asked.

Oh, oh, even they think he's going to die! I thought.

"Don't worry about getting a minister," I said. "My husband has made a commitment to Jesus Christ and so have I. Both of us have received him as our Savior. Paul doesn't need a minister. In fact, if there are any other patients here in the hospital who need spiritual help, I'd be willing to talk to them. If you don't think I can, you need to know that I've written a book about people who don't know how to be in the family of God. I tell them what the Scriptures have to say. That's my authority, since the Bible is God's Word." I nervously rattled on and on. I had not been to an emergency room before, so I didn't realize that everyone who registers is asked about his or her religious preference.

The girl at the desk looked at me and said in a serious voice, "*I* need your book."

"What do you mean?" I asked.

"I mean I need to read your book so I can know how to be in the family of God. I go to church but it's not been made clear as to what a person must do to be prepared for heaven."

"Oh, I'm sorry, our car is loaded down with suitcases and clothes. I don't think I can get at my books. But I'll sit down and write down God's requirements. I'll tell you exactly what the Bible says."

Other people were waiting in line behind me, so I couldn't take any more of her time. But I found a quiet corner and sat down to write. It had a calming effect on me. This is what I wrote:

We must first of all recognize that God is holy and his standard is perfection. We human beings are sinful and cannot reach God's standards. The Bible says that in Romans 3:23. It also says in Romans 6:23: "The wages of sin is death, but the gift of God is eternal life in Christ Jesus our Lord." The wonderful thing is, God didn't leave us to flounder but provided a way that we might be in his family. Romans 5:8 tells us that "God demonstrates his own love for us in this: While we were still sinners, Christ died for us." Jesus provided the way of salvation. He said, "I am the way and the truth and the life. No one comes to the Father except through me."

Knowing these verses is not enough. You must follow through by receiving Jesus Christ as your Savior. John 1:12 says, "Yet to all who received him [Jesus Christ], to those who believed in his name, he gave the right to become children of God." One more thing—you can't get to heaven by good works. It's not a reward for the good things we have done. Ephesians 2:8–9 tells us that salvation is by grace through faith—we can't do it ourselves. It's a gift God wants to give us if we receive Jesus Christ.

If you are ready to take this step, why don't you bow your head right now and thank God for sending his Son, Jesus Christ, to die on the cross for your sins. Then tell Jesus you want him to be your Savior.

It had been good for me to concentrate on someone else's need. I was perfectly at peace, just knowing that God had given me a work to do. In the midst of my anxiety about Paul, God drew my attention away from my own fears.

I went to the desk, handed the young woman my note, and said, "When we get to Florida, I'll send you a copy of my book *What Do You Say When?* Perhaps it will help reinforce what I have just written. The book contains stories of people just like you. I once met a woman in a swimming pool who didn't know how to pray. I met another woman on the tennis court who asked, 'Nellie, what makes you tick?' Another woman told me, 'I wish I knew God better.'"

"Thank you so much," the registrar said. "I really appreciate what you've done. It means a lot to me. By the way, my name is Maria. I would appreciate it if you would pray for me—that is, if you ever think of me."

"I've already prayed for you and will continue to do so. Now, is there some way I can find out about my husband's condition?" I asked.

"Ordinarily we don't allow anyone except hospital personnel in the treatment area, but go ahead. I'll call and tell them you're coming."

I appreciated her kindness. I walked through the double doors and greeted the nurse at the desk. "Has the doctor discovered the cause of my husband's problem? Is he going to be all right? Is he still in a lot of pain?"

The nurse gave me a big smile. "Yes, he's going to be fine. But first he has to get rid of the kidney stone that is causing the pain. We've sedated him and taken some X-rays. Let's see if he's awake yet.

"Mr. Pickard, you wife's here to see you," the nurse said, as we entered his cubicle. Paul was groggy and had a hard time opening his eyes.

"What's wrong with me?" he asked.

"You're going to be okay. You have a kidney stone," I said. "They are going to help you get rid of it. But I want you to know your pain hasn't been wasted. I had a chance to share the gospel with the woman at the front desk. She seems very responsive and would like a copy of my book. Is there any way I can get hold of one?"

Paul managed to say, "Underneath the clothes in the backseat is an open box. Lift up the clothes and. . . ." Then he went back to sleep.

I returned to the lobby and watched as a policeman brought in a gunshot victim. The young man's friends filled the room. Their faces appeared somber and tense. No one spoke.

Since it was two o'clock in the morning, I wasn't exactly eager to go to the parking lot alone. But I *had* to get the book! As I walked toward the door, I noticed the sheriff and a policeman standing in a corner. I approached them and asked whether one of them would be willing to go with me to my car so I could get a book I wanted to give to the registrar.

Southern hospitality rose to the occasion. "I think we can help you," the sheriff said. He motioned for the policeman to go with me after the two of them checked out at the desk.

When I opened the car door and reached under the clothing that was hanging up in the back, I had no trouble finding my book.

The policeman walked beside me as we went back to the hospital. "May I see your book?" he asked. I handed it to him and he browsed through it in the lobby.

"Lady, now I understand. You want her to know the Lord, right? My father is a minister and so was my grandfather. I like what you're doing."

I went to the desk and gave Maria the book. She thanked me and said, "I really appreciate your willingness to talk to me. I wish we could spend some time together, but I know that's impossible."

I encouraged her to start reading the Bible. "Start in

the Book of John. It will tell you who Jesus Christ is. You need to get to know him better," I said.

At four o'clock that morning, the hospital released Paul, with the condition that he see a doctor as soon as we got to Boca Raton. The doctor handed him a prescription for pain. "Stop at a drugstore in the morning and get it filled," he said. "You have to do it while you're in Georgia; otherwise it won't be honored. But if the pain gets intense as you travel, you had better stop at the nearest hospital."

We had about three hours of sleep and soon after dawn stopped at four drugstores. It was Sunday, so all were closed until noon.

"Let's keep going," Paul said. "We don't want to stay here another four hours."

Though I was concerned that Paul get his medicine, I took his suggestion and began driving. I drove from eight in the morning until two in the afternoon. Paul slept most of the way. I prayed, "Help us reach our destination without incident. Please keep Paul safe until we arrive."

When Paul awoke, he said, "I feel better. I feel like driving."

We reached Boca Raton at six that evening. Paul took our luggage upstairs and sat down to rest. All of a sudden the pain returned. I hurried to the drugstore and explained the situation when I showed the pharmacist the prescription. I asked if he could possibly honor it. He said, "Ordinarily we don't, because it's from out of state—but under the circumstances, I'll help you out. That is, if you promise to see a doctor the first thing in the morning."

God saw us through. Six days later, Paul passed the stone!

Postscript

Paul and I believe in God's divine appointments. They are always surprises, though we also know that we won't be exempt from life's difficulties. The Bible says, "Yet man is born to trouble as surely as sparks fly upward" (Job 5:7). But Hebrews 13:5 reminds us that God has said, "Never will I leave you; never will I forsake you." Sometimes God combines the two truths, so blessings often come out of hardships.

For Maria, Paul's medical problem meant an introduction into God's family and an answer she had been seeking. We would not have met her if God had not provided a reason for us to be at that hospital at that particular time.

Pain is never fun, but we praise God that Paul's pain wasn't wasted. And even the stones rose up to praise God!

*For bodily exercise profiteth little: but godliness
is profitable unto all things, having promise of the
life that now is, and of that which is to come.*

[1 Timothy 4:8 KJV]

5

In Need of a Little Exercise

I've finally finished my manuscript," I told Paul.
"Sitting at the word processor for hours at a
time is taking its toll on my body, not to mention those
delicious desserts at the retreats and seminars where
I'm invited to speak. I'm gaining weight and feeling logy.

"Joan tells me the mall opens two hours early every
morning just for walkers. I think I'll join her. Maybe that
will get me back in shape. Besides, I think I deserve some
time for myself, don't you?" I said with a hint of silliness.

"I agree," Paul said. "You do need some exercise.
You're still going to be available to share your faith,
aren't you?" he teased.

"Of course, but I even need a break from that once
in a while."

Walking was invigorating. I often met Joan and other people from church and walked with them. One morning I noticed a young woman reading a newspaper at a table in the eating area of the mall. As I passed by, she looked up and smiled, so I asked, "What are you reading?" Before she could answer, I noticed it was one of those tabloids seen at the supermarket checkout counters.

"Do you believe that stuff?" I asked.

"No, not really, but I enjoy reading about it. I buy this paper every week and come here to read before I start work."

"I read something a lot more exciting than that. Something that gives direction to my life and shows me how to have real fulfillment. I just love it," I said.

"And what's that?" she asked.

"I read the Bible every morning. It's a great way to start the day."

"You know, my mother says the same thing. Maybe I'll ask her to give me a Bible for Christmas."

"That's a great idea. It will do a lot more for you than the paper you're reading." I introduced myself and she told me her name was Sarah.

The week after Christmas I passed by the counter where Sarah was working. "I got my Bible for Christmas," she said as she held it up for me to see.

"Wonderful! I remember that you used to read the tabloid at the table over there. Do you have enough courage to read your Bible instead?" I teased.

"I . . . think so," she answered with some hesitation.

Early the following day I saw Sarah reading her Bible at her usual table. I walked a little longer, then sat down beside her and asked, "Do you know anything about Jesus Christ?"

"I used to go to Sunday school a long time ago, and I remember a few things. I need to know more about God, though," she admitted wistfully.

"The way to know God is through Jesus Christ," I said. "He came to earth to show us what the Father is like. Jesus said, 'I am the way and the truth and the life. No one comes to the Father except through me.'

"Sarah, when you went to Sunday school, did you ever hear the verse that says, 'For God so loved the world that he gave his one and only Son, that whoever believes in him shall not perish but have eternal life'? That's John 3:16."

"Yes, I've heard that before," Sarah answered. "But I'm not sure what it means."

I continued to share with her from Scripture. "It also says in Romans 3:23, 'For all have sinned and fall short of the glory of God.' That means that no one can reach God's standards, that the whole world stands guilty before God. Now let me tell you what it says in Romans 5:8: 'But God demonstrates his own love for us in this: While we were still sinners, Christ died for us.'

"But Sarah, you also need to know that even though you may do nice things, heaven is not a reward for good behavior. That's what it says in Ephesians 2:8 and 9. The solution is found in John 1:12, which says, 'Yet to all who received him'—Jesus, that is—'to those who believed in his name, he gave the right to become children of God.'"

After giving Sarah time to think about what I had said, I finally asked her, "Do you believe God when he says you are a sinner?"

"Yes, I know I am," she replied.

"Would you like to experience his love and forgiveness by receiving Christ as your Savior?"

"I surely would," she answered.

I helped Sarah pray. Right then and there she confessed she was a sinner and received Jesus Christ as her Savior.

"Even though I've heard some of these Bible verses before," she said, "I never made them personal, that is, meant just for me. I hope you will teach me more about the Bible." I promised I would.

I saw Sarah again the following week. She was excited as she told me that she and her boyfriend had gone to church on New Year's Eve. "I really enjoyed it," she said, "now that I know more about what it all means."

I gave her a Bible-study booklet, "The Uniqueness of Jesus," published by Campus Crusade for Christ. I asked her to look it over and said I would help her with her questions when she was ready.

The next time I saw Sarah, she looked troubled. "My brother died in his sleep last night," she told me. "He was only twenty-seven. I feel just awful. He was so young. I will have to be gone for several days. The funeral will be in Indiana."

I assured her of my prayers, knowing we would have to put the Bible study on hold for the time being.

Soon after that, as I was walking the mall with my friend Joan, she pointed to a woman walking across the aisle from us. "Roger is having a Bible study with that woman's husband this morning," she told me.

"What about her—is she a believer?" I asked Joan.

"I'm not really sure about Jane," she answered.

The following day Joan had a hair appointment, so I walked alone. When I noticed Jane walking ahead of me, I caught up to her and asked with a smile, "Do you know Joan Van Noord?"

"Yes, and I know Roger, her husband, too," she said. "They are such fine people."

"They attend our church," I said. Jane told me the name of her church and we got better acquainted as we walked together. When we passed the counter where Sarah usually worked, I told Jane the story of how we had met. "I hope to start a Bible study with her soon," I added.

To my delight and surprise, Jane asked in a hesitant voice, "Could I join your Bible study? I've been wanting to attend one for a long time. When I asked my pastor if he was interested in having Bible classes at the church, he said no."

"I would be delighted to get together with you. How about next Monday, before we walk?"

Before we started our study, I asked Jane if she had ever committed her life to Jesus Christ. "I'm not sure, but I'd like to" was her response. We prayed together, and she told the Lord she wanted him to be in control of her life. It was a moving moment for both of us.

Five days later, we met again and Jane said, "Last Monday was the highlight of my week. If I hadn't committed my life to Christ, I wouldn't have made it through the past few days."

"Tell me about it," I prodded.

"Well, it's been a very rough week. One of my relatives committed suicide. My daughter's husband left her and their eight children. And my cousin's husband has been diagnosed as having cancer. I was overwhelmed by all this news, but I am so grateful for the experience I had on Monday. With the strength that God is giving me, I am doing what I can to help my daughter and to encourage the others in their grief."

We've gotten together several times since, and Jane says, "I need this study. I want to learn more. I appreciate your help."

Because of my walks I was also able to witness to a young man from the bakery department at the mall. When he told me his name was Christopher, I said, "I like your name—especially the first part."

"You mean Chris?" he asked.

"Well, no, I mean Christ."

He smiled and then surprised me by saying, "Interesting you should say that. I've been thinking about Christ lately and wish I knew more about him. They don't teach much about him in church these days, do they?"

"They do in the church I attend," I said. "I'd like to give you a booklet I have in my purse. It will give you the basics of what Christianity is all about. Why don't you read it and see if it makes sense to you?"

"Thanks, I'd like to do that."

When I saw Chris later that week he said, "Thanks for giving me the booklet. It did make sense to me. I also prayed the prayer on page ten. And I received Christ as my Savior."

I was delighted and encouraged him to start reading the Scriptures. The next day he told me he had started to read the Bible from the beginning and had just finished the creation passages.

"I'd encourage you to start reading the Book of John

first. It's important that you learn more about Jesus Christ."

"I'll do that," Chris said.

When I saw Chris the following morning, he showed me a book he had picked up at a local bookstore. It was about the science of the mind. One quick look convinced me that the authors had distorted the Scriptures. They were false teachers. I told Chris the book was man-centered, not God-centered.

"I wondered about that," he said. "They write as though man, not Jesus, is the true vine."

"You've got it," I said. "I have plenty of books for you to read. You've started well, but you've got to stay on track."

Postscript

I also met a security guard at the mall. Her name is Linda. She is a fine Christian who has been involved in Bible-study groups for several years. Linda is willing to disciple Sarah and has already encouraged her to dig deeply into the Word.

Christopher is desirous of learning more about God and the Bible. Since I can only talk to him briefly over the counter and give him books to read, I asked him if he would be interested in a weekly Bible study.

"I'd be very interested," he said.

I called my friend Roger Van Noord, who is on staff with "The Navigators." He contacted Chris and they have made arrangements to get together regularly.

I'm very conscious of the networking that goes on in God's work. Some sow, some water, but only God can give the increase.

My actual walking time is sometimes shortened

because I can never let witnessing opportunities slip by. But that's all right. I do have a stationary bicycle at home that I can use to make up for my lack of exercise! And somehow I think I've shown that even bodily exercise can be profitable in terms of soulwinning!

[Jesus said:] "What good is it for a man to gain the whole world, yet forfeit his soul? Or what can a man give in exchange for his soul?"

[Mark 8:36–37]

6

Hotel Encounters

"A re the two men seated across from us speaking French?" I asked my husband as I glanced around the restaurant.

"I'm not sure," Paul answered. "But they sound like Frenchmen."

Our young waiter was standing nearby, waiting to take our order. He heard my question and said, "Actually they're speaking Italian."

"Is *your* background Italian?" I asked.

"No, Mexican. My parents live in Texas. I've been in this city only a few months."

"I should have known—I see your name is Juan, and that certainly isn't Italian."

"Juan is a Spanish name."

"I find this hotel fascinating," I said. "There are so many different nationalities represented here. They even have clocks on the wall behind the front desk that show the time in London, Tokyo, Singapore, and Moscow. You must serve a lot of businessmen from these countries."

"Yes, we take care of people from all over the world. Where do you live?" Juan asked.

"We're from Birmingham, Michigan. I'm here speaking at a women's retreat sponsored by radio station WBCL. It's connected with Summit Christian College."

"What do you speak about?" Juan asked.

"I'm here encouraging Christians to share the gospel of Jesus Christ. The world is a mess, and Jesus is the only hope for its confused and frightened people. Do you have a church background?" I asked.

"I was raised as a Roman Catholic," he answered. "But I'm not attending church at the present."

"I would like to give you a booklet that will give you an idea of what I talk about at these seminars. Would you read it and then—when I come back for another meal—tell me what you think? I'd like to know if it makes sense to you."

Juan took the booklet and said, "I'd love to read it, and I'll let you know what I think of it."

Paul and I ordered our meal. I made a point of telling Juan to serve me decaffeinated coffee so I would be able to get a good night's sleep.

The meal was excellent but I did have a hard time sleeping that night. I was sure Juan had forgotten my request and given me regular coffee.

The following evening we again visited the hotel's dining room. Some of the workshop leaders at the retreat were also there. When I saw Juan, I asked, "Did you get a chance to read the booklet?"

"Yes, I did," he said with great enthusiasm. "The best part was about receiving Jesus Christ."

I had often given someone this booklet (*The Four Spiritual Laws*), but never had I received such an energetic response. It was as though something had been settled in this young man's life. I wanted to be sure he understood, so I asked, "Did you pray and agree with God that you are a sinner and need Jesus Christ to save you?"

"I sure did. It felt good to receive Jesus as my Savior," he repeated.

"That's the best decision you'll ever make in your life, Juan. Now I'd like you to meet some of the new friends I met at the retreat." I brought him over to their table and said, "Juan, I want you to meet my friends. Each one has received Christ as Savior. Because their lives have been transformed, they are at the retreat encouraging other believers to be their best for God."

"Mrs. Pickard gave me a booklet explaining Christianity," Juan said. "The best part was receiving Jesus Christ. I'm happy to say, 'I did that.'"

"I'm so glad, Juan. But, by the way," I said teasingly, "I'm sure the last time I ate here, you gave me regular coffee instead of decaffeinated. I know because I didn't sleep. But I've forgiven you."

"It *was* decaffeinated, Mrs. Pickard. Perhaps you didn't sleep because you got so excited telling me about Jesus Christ."

Everyone had a good laugh, and I finally gave in and said, "You may be right."

Juan promised he would start reading in the Book of John. He appeared to be very sincere about his new commitment.

The following morning we had breakfast in the coffee shop. I told the waiter to be sure to give me decaffeinated coffee. "I'm still sure I was given regular the other night, because I couldn't sleep," I said to Paul.

"Why don't you sue the hotel? That seems to be part of the American way," joked the man sitting a few tables away.

I smiled and answered, "I don't believe in suing people." It was early in the morning and very few people were in the restaurant. My husband commented on the man's crisp accent and asked if he was from England.

"Yes, as a matter of fact I am. I'm on business here for Lloyd's of London. I travel all around the world. Sometimes my wife comes with me."

"Why don't you come over and join us?" I suggested.

"Thanks, but I'm used to dining alone."

The Englishman and my husband kept talking across the room, so I once again urged him to sit with us, adding, "Maybe we can learn from each other."

"I think I'd like that." Since his order had already been taken, he hailed his waiter and told him he had changed his seat.

We had a good time getting acquainted. Paul and our new friend talked about world conditions. We enjoyed hearing him speak. His accent was delightful, and he seemed to be full of knowledge in many areas of life.

"What is the spiritual tone in England these days?" I asked.

"Not very good. Our people aren't very inclined toward religion, and the church doesn't seem to meet their need."

"What sort of impact did Billy Graham's crusade have on the English?" I asked.

"I think it was a dud," he answered.

"That surprises me. I heard all kinds of good reports."

"Well, I didn't go for it," he replied.

"What about you?" I asked. "What is your religious background?"

"I was raised in the Church of England. Though I don't attend church regularly, I *am* a Christian. But I have problems concerning the way God runs things," he went on.

"What do you mean?" I asked.

"I don't think God is fair. He took my mother when she was only thirty-four years old. She was a good woman. It seems as though God takes the good people and rewards the bad ones. I just don't understand it. And what about the wicked rulers? Why does he allow them to live?" The Englishman then put his head in his hands and said, "I just don't understand. I can't figure out God's ways. I think he should let good people live and get rid of evil." He appeared very upset.

"Have you ever read the Bible?" I asked.

"Oh, I read it now and then."

"You remind me of a verse in the Bible that says, 'You turn things upside down, as if the potter were thought to be like the clay! . . . Can the pot say of the potter, "He knows nothing"?' That's from Isaiah 29:16. You are criticizing a God you don't know. The Bible is God's Word. Why not start reading it regularly?"

"Well, I'm not sure the Bible is true."

"You really surprise me. You are a well-educated and intelligent man. You are knowledgeable in so many things except the most important thing of all—God's Word."

Paul said, "You say you are a Christian. On what basis do you say that?" The Englishman didn't answer, but instead went on arguing the authenticity of the Bible.

"On what basis, then, do you think you are a Christian?" Paul persisted.

Our new friend bowed his head and quietly said, "Because I believe there has to be more to life than what I see in the world. I do believe—I just don't *know*."

Then I said, "I have written a couple of books about people who discovered God through the Bible. They put their trust in him and made him Lord of their lives. I'd like to give you my books if you promise to read them."

"Thank you very much. I know my wife will read them right away. Let me give you my card," he continued. "I would be pleased if you would call us if you ever get to London."

We all rode up on the elevator together. We pushed the button for the third floor. Our English friend, who took out a key for the penthouse suite, said, "Now *I* probably won't sleep tonight. You've given me a lot to think about."

Postscript

Such chance encounters as these provide an endless seedbed for sowing the Good News—the universal message of salvation that transcends cultural and national boundaries.

Juan, the young Hispanic waiter, was eager to receive Christ. All he needed was to know how. On the other hand, the English businessman was hurt and angry. He wanted to tell the Creator how to run his universe. As far as the world is concerned, this man is successful, but he is spiritually impoverished. He left a crack in the door, however, when he admitted that he probably wouldn't sleep that night! He accepted my books, knowing what the subject would be. Then he issued an invitation for us to call him if we get to England. The seed was cast. Now we pray that God will send someone to water it.

Therefore I will boast all the more gladly about my weaknesses, so that Christ's power may rest on me. That is why, for Christ's sake, I delight in weaknesses, in insults, in hardships, in persecutions, in difficulties. For when I am weak, then I am strong.

[2 Corinthians 12:9b–10]

7

But for the Grace of God

I was standing in the foyer of our church when I became aware that a pretty young woman was staring at me. I guessed her age to be about sixteen. She smiled and said, "I apologize for staring. You *are* Mrs. Pickard, aren't you?"

"Yes, I am. And what is *your* name?" I asked as I returned her smile.

"Jane Sears. My friend Laurie said you are involved in an arts and crafts class at the Christian school. She said you give devotions—or something. Can you tell me about that?"

I laughed and said, "Sally Roost teaches the crafts and I give a few thoughts from the Scriptures. We meet every Monday night at seven. Are you interested in attending?"

"Actually I'm hoping my mother will come," she answered.

"Tell your mom we'd love to have her."

Jane hesitated before saying, "I wonder—would you invite her? She promised to come to church next Sunday. I'll introduce you to her then." She started to walk away, but changed her mind and returned to ask, "May I come to see you after school one day next week? My mother needs a real friend, but first you need to know a few things about her." Jane's eyes told me this was important.

"Tuesday is a good day for me," I said. "I'll have some cookies and milk for you."

The following Tuesday at three-thirty, the doorbell rang. It was Jane.

"Thank you for letting me come," she said. "I love my mother very much, but she is not a Christian and—"

"Let's go out on the porch and enjoy our snack," I interrupted. "Then we can relax as we talk."

I put a few goodies on a plate and told her to help herself. She seemed anxious to tell me about her mother, so I said, "You say your mother is not a believer. Before we talk about her, would you tell me something about yourself? How long have you known Christ, Jane?"

"I accepted Jesus as my Savior last summer while visiting my aunt in Mississippi. Even though I've attended church since I was a little girl, I only went because it was expected of me. My aunt told me that we are all sinners and need Christ's forgiveness. She helped me understand that I had to receive him as my personal Savior. I'm so glad I'm committed to Christ. It's helped me to cope with life."

I couldn't help but smile. *This young girl hasn't lived long enough to know about life,* I thought. *But then, I don't know what her problems are.*

"Since you are a new believer, how did you find out about Southfield Christian?" I asked Jane.

"That's part of my story. It's really a miracle. Before I went to SCS, I attended a Lutheran school. That was a few years ago. Then I attended Kingswood, a private boarding school for girls. That was part of the judge's orders."

"I don't understand. What do you mean by 'the judge's orders'?"

"When I was thirteen years old, my mother had one of her breakdowns. It was a frightening experience. She woke me up early one morning and said, "You've got to get up. The house is on fire. We've got to jump out the window." She took my hand and pulled me toward the open window.

"Mother had been acting strangely, and since I didn't smell smoke, I didn't want to jump. I had to fight with her to get away. I ran out of the house and went for help. Later she didn't remember the incident at all. She was hospitalized and I went to live with my dad and my grandmother.

"Mom's really a wonderful person, but she's experienced many tragedies in her life. I don't think she ever got over the death of her father. She found him in the basement of their home. He had hung himself. She was only seventeen at the time, and my grandmother couldn't function after that. It was left up to my mother to care for her. It was a heavy load for her to carry and it took its toll. After a while, Mom married, but it was not a happy marriage. All these sad experiences were too much for her. She eventually had her first break-down. I was only five years old at the time."

"My, what suffering she has gone through," I commented.

"She was hospitalized for a while and seemed to recover," Jane continued. "I know this experience greatly affected her life. My parents divorced when I was six years old. That didn't help Mom's mental condition. She went into deep depression and tried to slash her wrists. She recovered again and did pretty well until I was thirteen. That's when she tried to jump out the window."

"You said you went to live with your father and your grandmother. How did that work out?"

"That was during my summer vacation. I believe if it wasn't for my grandmother, I wouldn't have survived. She loved me and took good care of me. She was a real lady. I loved being with her and wanted to be just like her. She had a maid who also was kind to me."

"What about your dad? How did you get along with him?" I asked.

"He drank a lot and talked against my mother all the time. I felt very uncomfortable with him. He said he hoped I would never go back to live with Mom. That hurt me."

"You know, Jane, you said earlier that accepting Christ has helped you cope with your problems."

"It has made all the difference in the world, Mrs. Pickard."

"I wondered when I first met you how a beautiful poised young lady could possibly have problems. Yet you appear to have everything under control."

Jane smiled and said, "That was partly due to the influence of my grandmother. And ever since I accepted Christ as my Savior, I can give him my worries and it keeps me calm. I know he will work all things for my good. As I look back, I can see how God provided for me each step of the way."

"Now back to the first question. How did you happen to attend Southfield Christian?" I asked.

"After Mom tried to jump out the window, she was hospitalized again. The courts took over and the judge decided I would be better off with Dad and my grandmother. But when she died, the maid contacted the judge and recommended that I attend boarding school. She didn't feel it would be good for me to live with Dad, since he was an alcoholic. You see, after Gramma died, my dad went off the deep end. He almost drank himself to death. That's when I went to Kingswood. Gramma left me a large sum of money, which took care of my schooling.

"Mom got better again and married the man who is now my stepfather. The judge said I had to visit Mom one weekend a month. We got along well. I knew she loved me and wanted me to be with her. I began to realize how much pain she had suffered in her life. I looked forward to those weekends.

"When I visited my aunt in Mississippi, I wrote Mom a long letter. I told her I wanted to come home and live with her. She was delighted, and I didn't have to attend boarding school any longer. The people next door told us about Southfield Christian. We visited the school and talked to the principal, who asked me privately why I wanted to attend SCS.

"'I'm a new believer and I want to be in a Christian

atmosphere,' I explained. I also told him about my mom. He said, 'I think this is just the school for you. We'd love to have you as a student.'"

"Have you told your mother that you've accepted Christ as your Savior?" I asked.

"Yes, I have. I told her as soon as I got home from visiting my aunt."

"What was her response?"

"She couldn't understand. She said, 'You've been going to church all your life. What's so different now?' Then I explained how I had only been going through the motions of being a Christian—that I didn't know Jesus Christ personally until recently.

"'I really don't understand what you are talking about,' Mom said. She didn't want to discuss it. That's why I asked you to invite her to the arts and crafts class. If you become friends, maybe you could explain it to her. I know she needs to accept Christ as her personal Savior."

"Well, that's quite a story you've told me," I said.

"I hadn't planned to tell you so much about Mom," Jane replied, "but now I'm glad I did. It will help you understand her better. She needs the Lord desperately. It would make such a difference in her life."

I promised to pray for Jane's mother and do what I could to become a good friend.

We next met in the foyer of the church the following Sunday. Jane brought her mother, as she had promised. At first I found her to be somewhat withdrawn, but she warmed up as we talked and got better acquainted. We discovered that both of us liked to work with our hands and especially enjoyed sewing and crafts.

"I've already told my mom about the arts and crafts class," Jane said with a big smile on her face.

"We'd love to have you come," I said to her mother. "I could pick you up. You're practically on my way to the school."

"I would like that very much," she said, "if it isn't too much trouble."

"No trouble at all. It's more fun than going alone."

Jane had introduced her mother to me as "Mrs. Brown." When I picked her up the following Monday, we decided to drop the formalities and call each other by our first names. So it was that Beverly and I first began our friendship.

The women in the class loved their crafts. The room was always buzzing with excitement as they compared their projects, and worked hard for an hour and a half. Then, after everything had been put away, I gave a fifteen-minute Bible study before we had our coffee and cookies.

One night I told the following story:

> Betty didn't know how to pray. Oh, she tried, but she felt God didn't hear her. I discovered that Betty didn't know Jesus as her Savior. "In order to reach God," I told her, "you have to come to him through Jesus Christ. According to Romans 3:23, we are all sinners. None of us can reach God's standards. But Jesus is perfect and without sin. Therefore, we can pray to God through him, but only if we confess that we are sinners and receive Christ as our Savior. First Timothy 2:5 says that Christ is our mediator and the only way to God. In other words, Jesus bridges the gap between God and man."
>
> "I get the picture," Betty said. "I need to acknowledge my sin and receive Jesus Christ as my Savior." And that's exactly what she did.

"Our time is up for tonight," I said. "Next week I'll tell you what happened to Betty's family as a result of her decision."

"May I bring you some coffee?" Beverly asked.

"Thanks, I'll clean up the table so we'll have room. Don't forget the cookies."

As we were sipping our coffee I asked Beverly, "Did what I said tonight make sense to you? Did you understand what I was talking about?"

"I understand now what Jane was trying to tell me when she came back from Mississippi. I couldn't figure out what had happened to her. But I see it all now. I've attended church ever since I can remember. I was taught that Jesus died on the cross for the sins of the world. But what you're saying is that I have to make this relationship personal. I have to admit that I have sinned against God and then I must acknowledge Jesus Christ as my Savior. I don't know why I didn't see it before."

"Would you like to do that right now?" I asked.

Jane's mother hesitated, then said, "I suppose now is the best time. But would you pray first?"

I thanked God for the Holy Spirit's work in our hearts. I also thanked him for dying on the cross for my sins and making me his child through my faith in Jesus Christ.

There was silence for a few seconds and then I heard Beverly pray, "I confess I am a sinner. I try to be good, but I can't help myself. I need Jesus Christ in my life and I accept him as my Savior. Thank you for helping me understand what it's all about. In Jesus' name, amen."

Beverly's face was radiant as she said, "I'll have to go home and tell Jane what happened tonight. She'll be so happy to know I've received Jesus. She tried to tell me I needed to have a personal relationship with Christ, but I just didn't understand."

"Jane did her part," I said. "God used her to prepare you for what happened tonight. She also has been praying for you. She loves you very much."

"She's a good kid. I can always depend on her to do what's right."

I suggested that Beverly start reading the Book of John. "Read the first chapter once every day. I'll give you some questions to work on. Look for the answers as you read."

When I picked up Beverly the following week, she seemed discouraged. "I have a hard time reading the Bible alone. I can't seem to find the answers. Could we do it together?"

"I have a suggestion. I've just received an invitation to conduct a series of Bible studies at a church on the east side of the city. If you come with me we could have lunch afterwards. Then we can discuss what you've learned." This arrangement worked out well. I enjoyed being with Beverly. We had a great time together.

"I learn so much more when you give the lesson and we discuss it than if I work on it by myself," she told me after a few weeks.

Jane stopped over one day, bursting with excitement. "I've got something to tell you."

"What's up? Tell me about it."

"I've never told you this before, but my father told me a long time ago, 'Jane, you are not to call your mother's husband "Father." He is not your father, so don't call him that. And please don't call him "Dad" either. Call him by his first name.'

"I felt that would be disrespectful," Jane continued. "And 'Mr. Brown' didn't sound right either. Do you know that for ten years I've never known what to call him. But something happened recently to change that. Actually it happened to me before it happened to him. I went to the young people's retreat last weekend. We were praying for the salvation of our loved ones. As I was praying for my stepfather, it came to me that perhaps I didn't love him. *How could I win him to Christ if I don't love him?* I thought. So I prayed that God would help me to love my stepfather and show that love.

"When I came home he was watching television. I knew better than to disturb him. When the program was over, I came up behind his chair, put my arms around him, and said, 'I don't think I've ever told you that I love you. I really do. Would you let me call you "Dad"?' I asked.

"'Yeah, sure, you can,' was all he said at the time. But last night after dinner he came to me and asked, 'Jane, do you mind if I call you my daughter?' I feel so good about it. Now I'm praying that God will work in his heart so I can talk to him about the Lord."

For a while, things went well for Jane's family. Then I began to notice a change in Beverly. She seemed to be groggy all the time and began to nod as we were talking. I sometimes thought she was going to fall asleep.

"Beverly, are you all right?" I asked one day.

"Oh, I'm sorry. I guess it must be my medication," she answered.

This happened so often that I decided to talk to Jane about it. "Your mom seems different lately. Why does she have to take so much medication?" I asked.

"I talked to the doctor about it and he just says, 'She needs it.' I wish he'd talk to Mom about that. I'm sure she's confused. It scares me. She acts so strange at times—like something is on her mind but she won't talk to me about it."

One day I got a call from the police, asking if I was acquainted with "a Beverly Brown."

"Yes, she's my friend," I told them. "Is something wrong?"

"You need to know she drove into her garage, closed the door, and left the motor running. She died of asphyxiation."

I was shocked! I felt as though someone had hit me in the stomach. "How did you get my name?" I asked.

"We found your name and phone number on a slip of paper in her purse. Did she call you today?" the policeman asked.

"I don't know," I said. "She might have called when I wasn't home."

I got in touch with Jane immediately. It was amazing how well she handled the situation. She had no thought for herself. Her main concern now was for the rest of the family.

I invited Jane's relatives to have dinner at our home after the funeral services. The deaconesses of our church brought most of the food. It meant a lot to the family to be together and comfort each other in their grief.

"Mrs. Pickard, would you be willing to tell my relatives how they can be saved?" Jane asked. "They may never get another chance to hear it."

"Well, I'd like to, but I'm not sure how to handle it," I told her. "I don't want it to seem awkward. But don't worry about it. God will show me a way."

After dinner, I invited the group to relax in the living

room. Then I said, "I'd like to tell you something about Beverly that most of you don't know. Perhaps it will be a comfort to you. Being related to Beverly, you know of the many mental breakdowns she has experienced. Her life has not been easy. In fact, to her it was overwhelming. About a year ago I had an opportunity to talk to her about what it means to be in the family of God—how she could have a personal relationship with Jesus Christ. She responded positively. I heard her pray and confess that she was a sinner. Then she received Christ as her Savior. None of us know the condition she was in when she closed the garage door and left the motor running. I don't think she knew what she was doing. I believe she is with the Lord today.

"This is a serious moment. We will all meet our Creator someday. What we do about Jesus Christ is the most important question we will ever have to face. I will close our time together with prayer. This might be a good time for those of you who have never received Christ to admit your sinfulness and receive Christ as your Savior."

Later, in talking to Jane, I said, "Your mother's death was a tragedy, but the pain need not be wasted. I'm sure your relatives have a lot to think about. God can use this experience in their lives. We'll leave the results up to him."

Jane's Christian friends were supportive. They rallied around her and included her in their activities. I was amazed at her composure.

"I'm determined to live for the Lord," she told me. "My family doesn't have a very good track record, but I'm not following in their footsteps. My path is ordered by the Lord, and that's the way I'm going to walk."

Postscript

Jane eventually married and moved to another state. Ten years went by before I saw her again. She is now a loving wife and happy mother of three beautiful children. We recently spent some time together and talked about God's dealings in our lives. She told me, "With the Lord's help, I hope to raise my children in a stable environment. My father died of alcoholism, my grandfather and my mother died tragic deaths—but I don't have to follow that pattern. My husband and I are committed to providing our children with a loving, healthy, and normal home. God is helping us to do just that."

Jane's changed life is a product of God's grace. I've spoken to many people who use their unhappy experiences to excuse their own failures. All of us have weaknesses, but Jesus said, "My grace is sufficient for you, for my power is made perfect in weakness" (2 Cor. 12:9).

A man is not a Jew if he is only one outwardly,
nor is circumcision merely outward and physical.
No, a man is a Jew if he is one inwardly; and cir-
cumcision is circumcision of the heart, by the
Spirit, not by the written code. Such a man's
praise is not from men, but from God.

[Romans 2:28–29]

8

All in the Family

"We got some more mail from the College of Jewish Studies today," my husband said. "Ever since I attended the mini-course in Hebrew they keep sending invitations to other programs."

"What are they offering now?" I asked.

"They have a four-session course on the meaning of the Passover. Would you like to go?" Paul asked. "Besides learning something new, maybe we can even contribute to the discussions."

"I'd like that," I answered. "We wouldn't want to offend anyone, but I wonder if we'll be allowed to ask questions. The Jewish people I've met seem to know so little about the Bible. Maybe this rabbi will be different."

We eagerly anticipated our first class. The rabbi, a young man with a pleasant personality, talked about the Seder, the Passover feast commemorating the exodus of the Jews from Egypt. First he explained the significance of preparing for it properly.

The cleaning of the house and the food and dishes to be used are all of utmost importance, but Passover is also a learning experience for the children. There are questions to be asked and answered pertaining to the deliverance of the Israelites from their slavery in Egypt. It is a time to joyfully thank God for intervening in history and freeing them from bondage.

The rabbi emphasized over and over that all leaven (yeast) was to be removed from the home and that no leavened products were to be eaten during this holiday period. This restriction referred to products made from wheat, barley, rye, or oats, such as bread and cake. When the Israelites fled from Egypt, there was no time to wait for bread to rise. Eating unleavened bread (matzos) at Passover was to serve as a reminder to the Jewish people of their escape.

Although our first session was very informative, I noticed that nothing was mentioned about how the death angel "passed over" the Israelites' homes—sparing those who obeyed God's command to put some of the blood of a lamb "without defect" on the top and side of the doorposts. This sign was crucial to the survival of their firstborn (Exodus 12:1–30). When the meeting was opened for questions I asked about this.

"We don't talk much about the blood," the rabbi said. "You see, the Jews have been accused of killing

Jesus. And some Jewish children even claim they have been told that Jews make matzos from the blood of Christians."

I was shocked at this statement and began shaking my head.

"You don't agree?" the rabbi questioned.

"I've never heard of such a thing."

When he looked at me, I sensed he had already known we weren't Jewish. I'm sure all doubt was removed after that exchange.

I went to the rabbi later and said, "My husband and I are Christians. We came to learn more about our Jewish neighbors. I want you to know we are very happy that the United States has sided with Israel. For God said, 'I will bless those who bless you [Abraham and his offspring], and whoever curses you I will curse . . .' [Gen. 12:3]. But if it offends you to have us here, we won't continue to come."

"Not at all. Please continue to attend," he answered graciously.

"You talked about getting rid of the leaven in the house," I said. "Does that perhaps also refer to the sin in our lives?"

"Well, we don't call it sin. We call it missing the mark," he said.

"Yes," I said, "sin is 'missing the mark,' and the Bible says a lot about that subject. I think it's important to discuss the Bible and learn about God's ways." I then looked at the rabbi and said, "I have several Jewish friends and neighbors with whom I would love to discuss the Bible. But I find they don't know the Scriptures very well, not even the five Books of Moses. That is very disappointing."

"You are right," the rabbi said. "And it's too bad."

On the way home, Paul and I talked about our new experience. We both felt it was worthwhile, for we were beginning to better understand the Jewish people.

I decided to bring my Bible with me the following week. The rabbi referred to the Book of Exodus several times, and I wrote down the passages he mentioned. I kept my Bible on my lap, not wanting to make a big deal about it. One of the men in the group came over to where I was sitting. He noticed my Bible and asked, "Is that a Thompson's Chain Reference Bible you have?"

I looked up in surprise and said, "Why, yes. How did you know?"

"I own one. It's very helpful." He then went back to his seat.

I must talk to that man afterward, I thought.

The group members also talked about inviting poor people and college students who would be away from home to their Seder observances. "You need to encourage people to ask questions, especially the children," the rabbi said. "Tell them the reason for the celebration: that God brought the Jews out of their slavery in Egypt. Emphasize that it is a time of gratefulness to God."

After the meeting, I asked the man who owned the Thompson's Bible how he happened to have it.

"I was traveling on an airplane," he said. "The man sitting next to me was reading the Bible. We got talking about it and he sent me a copy. I really enjoy reading it. By the way, I'm a cantor at a local synagogue, though I'm also involved with a family business. My name is Isidore."

I introduced myself and said, "How about reading Isaiah 53 this week? I'd like to discuss it with you next time." He wrote it down and said he would do it. Then he smiled and we parted.

I was eager to talk to the young cantor, but I never saw him again, for he didn't show up for the final two meetings. I'm praying that God will give him a hunger for his Word. I also pray that God will open his eyes and heart so he can receive the truth.

Our third session was held in the auditorium, where we were joined by the women's auxiliary. When I arrived, I noticed a young black man in his early twenties. He was preparing the coffee and tea and had arranged some delicious-looking cakes on the table. He smiled as I took my plate. "Are you Jewish?" I asked.

"No, I'm not."

"Are you a Christian?" I asked.

"I don't know. I belong to the sanctified church."

I wasn't sure what he meant, so I said, "Well, I'm saved and sanctified; 'sanctified' means set apart to God. But what does that word mean to you?"

"I'm confused about a lot of things," the young man admitted. "Our church worships on Saturdays and we follow God's law. I've asked three rabbis here how I can find God, but they tell me they don't know. I really need to find God. Nobody seems to know how."

I smiled and said, "The only way you can find God is through Jesus Christ. He died for our sins and was buried and rose again. Christ paid the penalty for our sins. Though he was sinless, he took our sin upon himself. When we confess to God that we are sinners and receive Jesus Christ as our Savior, we are saved from the penalty of our sinfulness. We then have a new and wonderful life in him."

The young man beamed as he said, "A light just turned on in my head. Somehow I know what you're saying is the truth."

"I'll bring you something to read next week," I said. "I

have to leave now. Class is ready to start. Think about
our conversation, and maybe next week we can talk a
little more."

"I'll look forward to it," he said. "By the way, my
name's Darica."

"I'm Mrs. Pickard. See you next week."

I prayed for my new friend all that week. I prayed for
an opportunity to make the way of salvation clear to him.

I was delighted to see Darica walking down the hall
as I entered the building the following week. "I have
something for you to read," I said. "It explains how you
can have a personal relationship with Jesus Christ.
Maybe we can talk after the meeting."

"I'd like that. You see, I'm afraid of going to hell. I've
got to find the way to God." Then shyly he added, "My
cousin died recently. He had AIDS. It scares me to
death."

"Have you been fooling around with sex?" I asked.

"No," he answered. "And I don't want to."

"Well, you won't have to worry about going to hell if
you know Jesus Christ as your Savior," I told him. "I'll
see you in about an hour."

The rabbi seemed eager to start our final meeting.
"We have a lot to cover today," he said. He then looked
at me and asked, "Did you bring your Bible today?"

"I meant to, but I forgot to put it in my bag," I said. I
was surprised at his question. I didn't realize he knew I
had brought it the week before.

"Well," he said, "I'm going to read from 1 Kings 18 today. Then we're going to talk about Elijah. Can anyone
tell me about Elijah?" he asked. No one answered. "How
did Elijah die?" the rabbi asked. Again no one responded, so I said, "He didn't die, God took him to heaven."

"According to 2 Kings 2:11, he was taken up in a whirlwind," my husband added.

"I figured you'd know," the rabbi said. Then he asked the rest of the group to read the story of Elijah at their Seder. "Don't read it from any book but the Bible. Read it from the Bible," he repeated.

I was happy to hear the rabbi emphasize reading the Bible. I was also glad I had talked to him previously about the Jewish people not being knowledgeable about the Scriptures.

When the meeting was over, both Paul and I thanked the rabbi for welcoming us into the group. Then I said, "At the first session you said that Christians blame the Jews for killing Jesus. You also said that Jews have been accused of making matzos from Christian blood. That hurt me. You see, I believe it was my sin and your sin that put Jesus on the cross. And I have never heard the untrue connection between matzos and the blood of Christians. A lot of people call themselves Christians, but that doesn't mean they are true believers. Anyone who honors Christ would never deliberately hurt a Jew."

"I could tell you were hurt that first week," he said. "I'm sorry."

Then we shook hands and I told him we felt attending the course had been worthwhile.

I found my new friend, Darica, eating his lunch in one of the classrooms. He grinned broadly when he saw me. "I received Christ as my Savior a few days ago," he said. "I'm so glad we met and that you could help me find the way to God."

"This is just the beginning of your new life. Do you have a Bible?" I asked. When he told me he did, I said, "It's important that you read a portion of it every day.

The Bible is God's Word. It's food for your soul. It will help you grow in the Christian life. I suggest you start reading in the Book of John. It will help you to know Jesus better. And I know you attend church, but if you'd like to visit ours sometime, we'd love to have you." I told him our location and the time of our service. He thanked me and I left.

A few months after we visited the Jewish Center, our pastor, Len Crowley, gave a series on the "The Last Act," which pertained to the promises God had given Israel. He did such an excellent job, that I decided to give the rabbi a tape of one of the messages. He received it well and thanked me. We had a good talk. I told him I planned to give him the rest of the tapes and hoped he wouldn't be offended.

While at the Jewish Center that day, I saw Darica again and asked him whether he was still reading the Bible.

"Every night," he answered." "A strange thing has happened since I've accepted Christ. Some of my old friends don't come around anymore."

"That's normal," I answered. "Not everyone will be happy about your commitment to Christ."

"That's all right with me," Darica smiled. "The most important thing is, I now know God through Jesus Christ. Thanks for your help."

Postscript

Paul and I felt we understood our Jewish friends a little better after attending these meetings. If we are to lead them to Christ, we need to be interested in their traditions. It is a great help to be aware of the Scriptures pertaining to their observances, because it's a good opener for a discussion. Although the Bible is the only source of truth, if we are to witness effectively to people, we must first show that we love them.

The young cantor intrigued me. I would have liked to talk to him further. I also wish I could meet the person who gave him the Thompson's Bible. May God bless him wherever he is.

Never could I have expected to have an opportunity to lead anyone to Christ in that Jewish Center. But God knew! That's what it means to be always available to God for witnessing. I never know when or where it will happen, so it is always a delightful surprise. People all around us are looking for answers. Believers have been given the privilege of spreading the Good News to all those who, like Darica, "need to find God."

The apostle Paul told the early church in Galatia that "there is neither Jew nor Greek, slave nor free, male nor female, for you are all one in Christ Jesus. If you belong to Christ, then you are Abraham's seed, and heirs according to the promise" (Gal. 3:28–29).

*[Jesus said:] "Therefore I tell you, do not worry
about your life, what you will eat or drink; or
about your body, what you will wear. Is not life
more important than food, and the body more
important than clothes?"*

[Matthew 6:25]

Temporal Riches
or Spiritual Blessings?

What can I say to my friend who watches
religious programs on television and sends
away for prayer cloths?" Barbara wrote. "The TV
preacher says the cloths are blessed and that she will
receive money as a result."

This was one of the questions sent to me when I was
on John DeBrine's radio program, "Songtime USA."

I answered Barbara by saying:

I, too, have friends who believe that God wants them
to be healthy, wealthy, and beautiful. But I don't see

that concept in the Scriptures. When the Bible talks about our blessings, it is referring to spiritual blessings. Ephesians 1 tells us that

1. God has blessed us in the heavenly realms with every spiritual blessing in Christ (v. 3).
2. He chose us in him before the creation of the world (v. 4).
3. In love he predestined us to be adopted as his sons through Jesus Christ (v. 5).
4. Through Christ's blood, we have redemption and the forgiveness of sins (v. 7).
5. God has made known to us the mystery of his will (v. 9).

This chapter of Ephesians goes on to say that we were chosen "for the praise of his glory," when we believed the truth of the gospel. We are then sealed with "the promised Holy Spirit, who is a deposit guaranteeing our inheritance . . ." (vv. 13–14). All these are spiritual blessings, not financial rewards. Our inheritance through Christ is incorruptible and can never fade away. Though we can't take our money or possessions with us when we die, we have something far better when we belong to God in Christ—the eternal treasures of his kingdom.

Share this passage in Ephesians 1 with your friend and explain to her what real riches are. Show her the difference between temporal pleasures and spiritual blessings. If she has not yet committed her life to Christ, invite her to receive him as her Savior.

Stan's attitude was a refreshing contrast to that of Barbara's friend. This young man was constantly looking for opportunities to honor the Lord. When he introduced himself to me at church one day, he said, "I enjoyed reading your books. Since I'm planning to do some free-lance writing, I'd like to talk to you about it. Would you be free for lunch one day next week? Perhaps you could give me some leads as to whom I should contact in the Christian publishing field. And I'd also like to discuss some other aspects of writing with you."

I met Stan the following Wednesday at a local restaurant. He was eager to tell me about his desire to write, but first I asked him what he did for a living.

"I don't have a job right now," he said. "I've recently been director of training and development for a large agency here in the Midwest. My company became involved in a corporate reorganization, and my job lasted for only fifteen months. Now I'm hoping to have time to do some writing.

"My former employer hired me to set up a training department to develop video discs. They had a large contract to fulfill, and I had experience in that line of work. The company had some problems. They knew very little about video discs and had a reputation for burning out their employees. Though I knew the job wouldn't give me a chance to attain my professional objectives, they offered me a good salary and many benefits. I even suspected that I might not last a year, but I hoped to be a light in that dark place. It would be a real challenge.

"I was eager to get started, but I soon discovered that their management style was far different from mine. I tried to change that in my department, only to be told I had to follow company policy."

I asked Stan whether he had a good working relationship with his employees.

"Yes, I did," he said. "I tried my best to encourage

them. During the first nine months, my staff worked hard to bring some order to the chaos and we made great progress. Although upper management had its doubts, my team was brilliant and enthusiastic. But there was always a sense of frustration, because the corporation was slow in approving the goals we had established."

"In spite of your frustration at work," I asked, "were you able to get across to your staff that you were a believer?"

"I'm sure I did. I kept my leather-bound Bible on my desk at all times because I wanted to make it obvious that it was the standard in my life. Besides, I needed to remind myself that I was an ambassador for Jesus Christ and must at all times guard my words and actions. I also put a number of Christian books on the credenza in my office. *Mere Christianity* by C. S. Lewis was borrowed several times. Orel Hershiser's *Out of the Blue* and Philip Yancey's *Where Is God When It Hurts?* found their way to several unsaved employees. And I made available some videotapes from James Dobson's 'Focus on the Family' film series. Many of the people who worked for me stopped by my office for counseling.

"A year after the job started, I knew the end was in sight. Upper management was not committed to change. Many times I was asked to take positions on personnel issues with which I didn't agree, but there was nothing I could do."

"What finally happened?" I asked.

"After thirteen months the training experiment was over, but it took two months for management to decide on the final reorganization. During that time there was considerable unrest among the employees. When the decisions were finally made, I was the first to discover that my department and my job would be eliminated. I was given two weeks' notice."

"How did you feel about that?" I asked. "Did you feel you had wasted more than a year of your life?"

"No, I joined the company knowing I might only last that long. My chief concern was how I would spend my final two weeks on the job. Since my greatest desire was to honor God, I wanted to make that time count for him. I wasn't as concerned about losing my job as I was for the men and women working under me. Some of them would be transferred, others might be out of work. The new structure wouldn't be announced for another month, so the place was in turmoil.

"I scheduled one last departmental meeting and prayed, 'God, help me to make the most of it for your sake.' Ideas kept flooding my mind. I laughed as I posted a sign for our final meeting. It said, 'Principles of Success in Problem Situations.'"

Stan told me he was amazed at the large turnout. This is how he described the meeting:

I started by saying that I wanted to share with them my definition of success. Besides the projector and my overheads, I kept my Bible on the table hoping its presence alone made a statement.

First I projected a drawing of a man standing before a river labeled "River of Decision." There were two bridges across that river. Across one bridge was bitterness, anger, gossip, (deceit), and revenge. Across the other lay kindness, humility, forgiveness, and consideration. "Which bridge would make working here more enjoyable?" I asked. "And which bridge would help an employee be more successful?" I wanted them to think about what constituted success or failure.

Next I put up a series of overheads that listed twenty-two of our major achievements. "You see," I told them, "we have already been successful here. Success is an ongoing process, not a point on a graph. We can all continue to be successful, even in the face of insurmountable odds."

Then I shared with the group my principles of success in life:

1. Be kind to each other. "Do to others as you would have them do to you"—Luke 6:31.

2. Be humble and forgiving. "Do not judge, or you too will be judged. For in the same way you judge others, you will be judged, and with the measure you use, it will be measured to you"—Matthew 7:1–2.

3. Be considerate of others. "Do nothing out of selfish ambition or vain conceit . . . look not only to your own interests, but also to the interests of others"—Philippians 2:3–4.

I reminded them that when I started at the agency, things were in chaos. "But now," I said, "after fifteen months, my supervisors and I have written and implemented a set of standards. Each of you has a ring binder that has provided direction and guidance on just about every aspect of video-disc development. By now you probably have guessed principle number four: Study the 'Standards and Conventions Document.' Here I am not referring to video-disc production. I am talking about the Bible. '. . . meditate on it day and night . . . do everything written in it. Then you will be prosperous and successful'—Joshua 1:8."

Then I went on to say, "The more you read the Bible, the more creative and freeing ideas will come to your mind. The words and ideas are so eternal and true that you will find them rearranging your priorities. If you are immersed in the Bible, you will get through all the storms of life safely."

They were hearing this from a guy who had just been caught in an organizational shape-up. If I could lose my job and keep my sanity, they could keep cool and be successful. Because the key was where they put their trust and ultimate faith, I told them about principle number five: Trust God in everything. "Trust in the LORD with all your heart and lean not on your own understanding . . . acknowledge him, and he will make your paths straight"—Proverbs 3:5–6.

"If we put our trust in management," I explained, "we may be disappointed. Trusting in the Creator of the universe is the most sensible approach."

I encouraged the assembled group to persevere in those principles of success. I finished with Romans 5:3–5, which tells us to "rejoice in our sufferings, because we know that suffering produces perseverance; perseverance, character; and character, hope. And hope [of the glory of God] does not disappoint us."

I ended my talk by congratulating my employees for their achievements and thanking them for their loyalty and hard work. For me, this meeting was the highlight of my fifteen months at the agency, but I was surprised at the applause! As they left, most of the workers shook my hand. I felt as though church had just been let out and I was the preacher.

"What a beautiful story!" I said to Stan. "I commend you for your courage in speaking out for the Lord. I would guess that you have been blessed over the years in seeing a number of business associates turn their hearts to God."

"Yes, I have. In fact, just recently a young man I had hired the previous year invited me out to dinner. As we were eating, he told me he owed me a lot. Tears came to my eyes when he told me he had rededicated his life to God because of my example. Seven months earlier, he had returned to church and was now taking membership classes. For the opportunity of turning people toward God, I would gladly lose my job again and again!"

Then Stan added rather shyly, "Mrs. Pickard, I've been telling you about myself. Actually, I came here to find out about your writing. How did you get started?"

"That was the biggest surprise of my life," I told him. "I had no real desire to be a writer, but God *did* give me a desire to share my faith. When many people came to Christ as a result, I was so excited about what happened that I began telling my friends about it. They kept after me to write about my experiences. My husband nagged me into going to a writers' conference. Then God used my writing teacher to convince me that my stories should be published.

"God's ways are mysterious. But I know he works everything out for his glory and our good if we trust him," I said.

Postscript

Stan and I talked several times after that about making contact with editors. I stressed the importance of sending query letters giving the publishers an idea of his work. He did agree with me that the most important part was to ask God for wisdom and direction in his writings.

The contrasting ideas about "success" in these two stories can be easily seen. The woman who sent in for prayer cloths wanted to gain temporal riches promised by a televangelist who used gimmicks. Instead of giving his listeners the Bread of Life, he gave them stones. (See Matt. 7:9.)

My young friend, Stan, was not seeking material wealth but the voice of the Father saying, "Well done, thou good and faithful servant." Stan doesn't know what the future holds for him in the field of writing. He does know, however, that God will lead him all the way.

For it is by grace you have been saved, through faith—and this not from yourselves, it is the gift of God—not by works, so that no one can boast.

[Ephesians 2:8–9]

10

For Such a Time as This

Our mail delivery has been spasmodic of late. This can be irritating, especially if I'm looking for an important piece of mail. I sometimes make several trips to the letter box, only to be disappointed.

We live in a townhouse, and our mailboxes are situated around the corner from our home. One nice thing about this is that we often meet neighbors and chat as we wait for the postman. One day I met a woman pushing a pretty little girl in a stroller. The child smiled brightly and said, "Hello."

"Hello there," I responded. "And what is your name?"

"Al—sandra."

"Is this nice lady your mommy?" I asked.

"She's my nanny," she answered proudly.

"Her name is really Alexandra," the woman said. "She's not quite three years old. That's a big name for such a little girl, isn't it?"

"Maybe someday she'll shorten it to Alex or Sandra," I commented. "But Alexandra is a pretty name; it sounds sort of musical."

I introduced myself and the woman told me her name was Eve.

"Are you new in the neighborhood?" I asked. "I haven't seen you before."

"Yes, I am. I started to work for Alexandra's mother two weeks ago. I'm from Vermont. I work for an agency and asked to be transferred out of state because I just had to get away. I'm trying to sort things out in my life. This has been a very hard year for me," Eve said sadly.

"You sound like you're hurting. I know I'm a stranger to you, but would it make you feel better if you talked about it?" I asked.

"I usually don't talk about my problems. But you seem so kind, and I need to talk to someone. It would be a welcome relief," she said with a smile.

"If I can help you in any way, I'd like to be available."

"I have no one but this child to talk to all day long," Eve told me. "Alexandra's mother and father both work. After dinner I go to my room so the parents can be alone. They are very nice to me, but I spend most of my evenings that way, even though they gave me the use of a car and told me I could have the evenings off. Of course, when they go out to dinner I have to baby-sit."

"Where do you go on your evenings off?" I asked.

"I don't go anywhere. I don't know my way around, so I wouldn't dare go out at night. I'd never find my way back home."

"Do you have a family?" I asked.

"Yes, I have four children in Vermont. My youngest daughter is with my mother right now. I thought getting away for a while would help me. I need to straighten things out in my mind. My troubles started when I discovered my husband had cheated on me. Then he began physically abusing me. He is a big man and very strong. He has hurt me many times, which is why I came out here to Michigan. I was afraid of him, but now I'm so lonesome I can hardly stand it," she added.

"Do you have a church background?" I asked her.

"Yes, I do," Eve said. "But I'm very disappointed in the church I've attended most of my life. Recently they started playing rock and roll music. I don't think that belongs in a church. And I saw my pastor buying liquor. I don't understand that. I don't want to go back, but I don't know where else to go."

"I attend a very fine church," I said. "It is probably not your denomination, but I'd love to have you come with my husband and me on Sunday. You'll meet a lot of wonderful people."

"I'd love to go, but I have to work Sunday morning," she said.

"Well, we have an evening service."

"I'll go anyplace," she laughed. "I need to get out of the house."

When we picked up Eve the following Sunday evening, she appeared entirely different from our first encounter. She had obviously dressed very carefully and had a refreshing radiance about her.

I introduced Eve to many of my friends at church. She was charming and outgoing. For the moment she seemed to have forgotten the pain she was carrying.

"I enjoyed the service very much," she said afterward. "I'd like to come again." I told her we'd be happy to pick her up for church anytime.

On the way home, I asked Eve whether she had visited any of the malls in our area. "No, I haven't," she replied. "I'd like to get some shoes, but I don't know where to go."

"I have time this week," I said. "I'd love to take you shopping and show you some of my favorite places." Eve seemed excited about the prospect, so we made a date to visit a couple of malls and several stores. She found the shoes she wanted and bought a couple of gifts for her friends back home. We had a good time and were becoming better acquainted.

Eve took Alexandra for a walk every day, usually ending up in the picnic area of our subdivision. It's a beautiful place, located in a ravine with a stream running through it.

"I love to sit and look at the water," Eve mentioned one day. "It's so peaceful. Why don't you come down sometime and we can talk?"

"I'm free tomorrow," I told her. "I'll meet you after lunch."

I liked Eve. She had high standards and we had fun together. I wanted very much to present the claims of Christ to her. *Tomorrow will be a good time to find out where she stands,* I thought.

The following day was beautiful. The sun was shining and I was looking forward to seeing my new friend. I prayed for wisdom, as I didn't want to offend her in any way. I knew Jesus Christ could meet her needs. He would see her through the hurt and pain in her life.

Eve and Alexandra were sitting at a picnic table by

the stream when I arrived. "Isn't this a wonderful place?" Eve said. "Vermont is beautiful, but this part of the country is lovely, too."

As I sat down, she said, "You told me you were going to speak in Grand Rapids next week. Tell me all about it. What are you going to talk about?"

"Well, I speak about our relationship to God. A lot of people have gone to church for years but don't know how to be a part of his family. I tell them what the Bible says. It's the only authority we have about God. Tell me, Eve, have you received Jesus Christ as your personal Savior? Do you believe he died for you *personally*?"

"I'm not sure, but I've tried to live a good life and be kind to people. I do my best," she said.

"Those are fine qualities," I said, "but that is not enough. You see, God sent his only Son, Jesus Christ, to die for our sins. Since the Bible says, 'For all have sinned and fall short of the glory of God,' we know that none of us can make the grade. Only Jesus is perfect. That puts us in a dilemma. Let me show you a little booklet. I'd like to read it to you and then I'll let you keep it." Then I showed her *The Four Spiritual Laws*.

We talked about the fact that we are separated from God because of our sin. And that "the wages of sin is death"—spiritual separation from God. I told her that the wonderful thing is: "God demonstrates his own love for us in this: While we were still sinners, Christ died for us" (Rom. 5:8). But he was buried and raised on the third day; Peter and the other disciples saw him, and more than five hundred people were witnesses to his life after the resurrection (1 Cor. 15:3–6).

"Eve," I continued, "Jesus said, 'I am the way and the truth and the life. No one comes to the Father except through me.' That's in John 14:6. He didn't say, 'I'll show you the way.' He said, 'I *am* the way.' But it isn't enough to know these facts. We must each receive Jesus Christ as our Savior. John 1:12 says, 'Yet to all who received him, to those who believed in his name, he gave the right to become children of God.'

"Another verse you need to know is Revelation 3:20. Jesus says, 'Here I am! I stand at the door and knock. If anyone hears my voice and opens the door, I will come in and eat with him, and he with me.' Jesus wants to be in your life, Eve. He wants you to trust him and have fellowship with him. He wants you to depend on him and accept his guidance. You don't have to bear your burdens and problems alone. He is waiting for your answer. Do you want him to be Lord of your life?" I asked.

Eve bowed her head and said, "Yes, I do want Christ in my life."

I helped her pray, and she received Christ as her Savior. What a beautiful time we had together.

"Strange how we met, isn't it?" Eve commented happily.

"God works in mysterious ways. You came all the way to Michigan so you could be introduced to the Savior! I believe God brought you here for such a time as this."

I gave Eve some Christian literature to read and told her to start reading the Book of John.

"I'm invited to a baby shower for one of my missionary friends. Would you like to come with me?" I asked.

"Are you sure it will be all right?"

"I'm sure it will be fine. But I'll call and double-check. Inell, the expectant mother, is a good friend. She's home on furlough from Africa and will be returning when the baby is ready to travel. Meeting people is her specialty, so she'll love getting acquainted with you."

Later I called to make sure the hostess would be prepared to have an extra guest. "No problem," she said. I explained that Eve was a brand-new babe in Christ. It would be good for her to be with other believers.

The shower was lovely and we had lots of fun. Several women came to our table and wanted to be introduced to Eve. I was delighted when Debbie, Inell's sister-in-law, who is also a missionary, showed special interest in Eve. She spent considerable time talking to her, making her feel welcomed and accepted.

Even though I had told Eve she didn't have to bring a gift, she had gone shopping with Alexandra and her mom and found some lovely embroidered bibs for the baby. This helped her feel more a part of the group, and Inell was touched.

Postscript

Eventually Eve felt ready to go back to Vermont. She missed her children, other family members, and old friends. She was stronger and ready to face whatever problems were ahead—because she now had the Lord as her guide.

Eve has been gone for several months now, but I've talked to her on the phone a few times. Her husband is back home again. "There are still problems," she said. "But if you want a home bad enough, you will be willing to bear the pain as you work them through with God's help." She also told me that she and her mother had visited four different churches. They liked a particular Baptist church very much. I pray they will get established in a Bible-believing church and have fellowship with other believers.

I constantly marvel at God's grace and his love for humankind. It's interesting how I met Eve. The mailbox is a friendly place and provides an easy way to get acquainted. Ephesians 5:16 speaks of "making the most of every opportunity, because the days are evil."

Opportunities for witnessing are everywhere. If you tell God you are available to him, he will show you where they are.

[Jesus said:] "You are the salt of the earth. . . .
You are the light of the world. . . . let your light
shine before men, that they may see your good
deeds and praise your Father in heaven."

[Matthew 5:13a, 14a, 16]

11

Salt and Light

I called the health-food store's manager to inquire about their sale on vitamins. "I notice you are advertising bee pollen. What is that supposed to do for a person?" I asked.

The man hesitated for a second, then said in a laughing voice, "You'll live forever; yep, you'll live forever."

"I know you're joking," I said. "But I *know* I'm going to live forever, and not because I buy your bee pollen. I plan to come to your store tomorrow and I'll tell you why I'm so sure."

"I'd like to hear about it," he said. "I'm really interested in why you think you're going to live forever. I'm going to be in and out of the store tomorrow. If I miss you, please leave your message with one of the clerks."

The man seemed congenial. *I'll go in the store tomorrow and tell it like it is,* I thought.

The following day, I went to the health-food store. I asked for the manager but was told he wasn't in. "Do you want to leave a message?" the clerk asked.

"Well, yes," I answered. "Please tell him that the woman who said she was going to live forever came in to see him. Tell him it isn't because of any vitamin or food product I eat. I know he was teasing when he said that eating bee pollen would make a person live forever. But I want you to tell him that *I* was serious."

The clerk looked at me skeptically. "I'm interested, too," he said. "How do you know you're going to live forever?"

"I know because I've accepted Jesus Christ as my personal Savior. There's a verse in the Bible that describes Jesus' prayer to the Father shortly before his crucifixion. This is what he said: 'Now this is eternal life: that they may know you, the only true God, and Jesus Christ, whom you have sent.' Those words are in John 17:3."

"You'd sure shock the manager if you told him that," the clerk said.

"It's God's truth," I said. "People need to know that God made a provision for their sin. If you confess you are a sinner and accept Jesus Christ as your Savior, God will let you into his heaven. Then you'll live forever with him. That's the Good News I want you to tell your boss."

The clerk tried to change the subject by saying, "I don't believe in God. I'm my own god, the only one in charge of my life."

"I can't believe what you're saying," I commented. "How can you say such a thing?"

"Well, whether I'm godly or ungodly, I make my own choices."

There was a young girl standing nearby. She also worked in the store and was listening to our conversation. I turned to her and asked, "What do you think about this man's statement? He thinks he's the god of his life."

"Well," she said, "if he *was* God, he'd never get sick—and he does. He has problems with his legs and other ailments, too. So it doesn't make much sense for him to say he's God. He obviously doesn't understand about *our* God."

What a perfect answer, I thought. *She sounds like a Christian.*

"Are you a believer in Jesus Christ?" I asked.

With a radiant smile she said, "I certainly am. Jesus is my Savior."

The male clerk then said, "I know I'm going to hell when I die. I really don't mind, because I'll be there with my friends."

"But in hell there is utter darkness," I said. "You won't be having a good time or living it up with your friends. You won't even see your friends. You'll be miserable. You'd better make things right with God before you die. If you die without knowing Jesus Christ, you're lost. You need to have him forgive your sins and must know him as your Savior before it's too late."

He shrugged his shoulders and said, "I'll take my chances."

As I walked out of the store, I thought, *How sad.* Later I prayed that the Spirit of God would remind him of our conversation and that it would trouble him. I continue to pray that he will ask the Christian girl in

the store more about the true and living God. And I
plan to visit the store again!

A couple of months after this incident, I met my
friend Connie.

"I heard you just got back from visiting your fiancé in
California. How was your trip?" I asked.

"I had a wonderful time. I'd like to tell you what happened on the way home. I was in a good mood when I
got on the plane, full of good will toward everyone. As I
sat down, my seat partner said, 'I just discovered that an
old friend of mine is on the plane. We haven't seen each
other in years. Would you mind trading seats with her?'

"'Not at all,' I said. 'I hope you have a wonderful visit
catching up on old times.'

"As I approached the section where I was to be
seated, I had second thoughts. I discovered that my new
seat was in the smoking section. The air was blue with
smoke, as though everyone had decided to light up at
once."

"That would be hard for me to handle," I interrupted.
"I get a coughing spell every time I'm around anyone
who smokes. What did you do?"

"Though I wasn't happy about it, I decided to make
the best of the situation. Then I prayed, 'Lord you know
how much smoking bothers me. If you have some purpose in this setup, I'm available to you.' I began to feel
better.

"I sat down and introduced myself to my new seatmate. She in turn said, 'I'd like you to meet my husband, George. My name's Hilda.'

"I told them that I wasn't supposed to be sitting in
that section and explained why I had traded seats.
When I commented, 'Isn't the Lord good to give us such

wonderful weather?' the woman looked at me strangely as though she didn't know what I was talking about. She told me she didn't know anything about the Lord and that her husband was an atheist.

"'Changing seats couldn't have been a mistake after all,' I said. 'I'm sure God meant for me to sit next to you. I'd like to tell you something about God and how you can know him as I do.'"

"How did the woman respond?" I asked Connie.

"She was polite as I began telling her that God loved us so much he sent his only Son to die on the cross for our sins. She seemed interested, so I continued with our conversation. I said, 'I believe this situation was an appointment arranged by God.'

"'Do you really think so?' she answered. She seemed surprised but touched.

"'You mean that God would care enough that he'd arrange for us to have conversation together?'

"'Absolutely,' I said. Time went quickly as I continued to talk about God's love for all mankind. When we landed, I said, 'I hope we'll meet again. And I hope your last flight will be to heaven.'

"'Well,' the woman smiled, 'I don't think it's fair to come to God when I'm in a jam. If I haven't trusted him up until now, I don't think it would be right. I don't want to be rude.'

"I looked at her and said, 'But God wants us to come to him anytime—even if we're crying for help. He's waiting for you to call on him. He's always there. I'm praying that you will come to know God as I have.'"

"Connie," I said, "you took what might have been an unpleasant experience and turned it into a blessing. I'm sure that pleased the Lord."

Postscript

There are confused and needy people all over the world. Opportunities to spread the light of the gospel are everywhere. We just need to open our eyes and ears to the possibilities of sowing the seed of God's Word. He will give the increase.

Witnessing is a mind-set. God has provided every believer with spiritual antennas so that we can pick up on a person's remarks and respond with a biblical truth. The manager of the health-food store jokingly said, "Bee pollen will make you live forever." As soon as I heard that phrase, "live forever," I took it as an opportunity to explain what Jesus said about eternal life.

Connie wondered if she had spoken too quickly when she gave up her seat. Then she realized it was providential. It was God's divine appointment, and it gave her a chance to talk to her seatmate about the Lord.

When Jesus Christ is Lord of our lives, he puts a desire in our hearts to obey him. Jesus said, "As the Father has sent me, I am sending you" (John 20:21b). And he also said, "But you will receive power when the Holy Spirit comes on you; and you will be my witnesses . . . to the ends of the earth" (Acts 1:8). That's a comforting verse for the believer, for in ourselves we are weak and timid.

We are called to be both salt and light in the world. Salt, being a preservative, keeps food from spoiling. By the same token, Christians preserve God's truth and help keep a lid on evil and corruption. We also function as beacons of hope in a dark world—because we reflect Christ, who *is* the light of the world (John 8:12).

Do not be anxious about anything, but in every-thing, by prayer and petition, with thanksgiving, present your requests to God. And the peace of God, which transcends all understanding, will guard your hearts and your minds in Christ Jesus.

[Philippians 4:6–7]

12

Christmas Coffees

Would you be willing to be one of the speakers at our Christmas Coffees?" my friend Lauren asked.

"Christmas Coffees? I don't know anything about them," I said. "I've been speaking on the East Coast for the past few weeks. I've probably missed a lot. Tell me about them."

"The women of the church have been encouraged to invite their neighbors to their homes during the holidays," she said. "It will be an opportunity to share the real meaning of Christmas and show love to those who live near us. Someone will also present an inspirational

117

message, and the people attending will be given an opportunity to receive Christ. Your name came up as a possible speaker. Would you be willing to help?"

"I'd love to be involved," I said. "I think it's a great opportunity to reach our neighbors for Christ. Was this your idea, Lauren?" I asked.

"Actually, my friend Jeanie read about a church in Minnesota that's been having Christmas Coffees for several years. Their church members host about two hundred such gatherings every year. The results have been astounding. We decided to present the idea to the ladies of our church. Even though some of the women are timid about inviting their neighbors, they're willing to get involved. I'll give you the telephone numbers of your hostesses so you can call and get directions to their homes."

When I called Pam, one of my hostesses, to confirm my commitment, I reminded her that I would be giving the guests an opportunity to receive Christ as Savior at the end of my talk. "We'll trust the Lord for the results," I said.

There was dead silence. I thought we'd been disconnected. "Are you still there?" I asked.

"Yeah," she said hesitatingly. "It's just that I'm not comfortable having you give an invitation. You see my mother is coming and she said, 'If it gets too heavy, I'll leave right in the middle of the program.' That makes me very nervous, so I'd prefer you didn't give an invitation."

"Pam," I answered, "I didn't set up the program. If I'm to do this, I'll have to follow the planned format. Don't worry, I won't collar anyone. I'll just share how I began to understand the real meaning of Christmas. Perhaps some will identify with my experience."

The following day I got a call from Pam's co-hostess, Becky, who said, "Pam would like us to meet for coffee and discuss the meeting. She's concerned about her mother and is still hesitant about your giving an invitation. I think it will be just fine, but for her peace of mind perhaps we'd better get together."

"Why don't you come here on Wednesday?" I offered. "It will be better than going to a noisy restaurant."

Wednesday morning I got a call from Pam. "I won't be able to meet with you. Mother is having some chest pains and I have to bring her to the doctor. But Becky will come."

"We'll be praying for your mother," I said. "God can use this to remind her that earthly life is short and we need to prepare for the hereafter. Remember, Pam, God's in control. We need to trust him."

I didn't know Becky well. I had met her briefly at an autographing party. She had recently moved into Pam's neighborhood and the two of them were just getting to know each other. They had become acquainted through car-pooling their children to the same Christian school. Becky's husband was the new president of Tyndale Bible College. I had heard him speak and was impressed by his interest in evangelism. He told us that his wife had been involved with Campus Crusade and had a heart for sharing the gospel. I was looking forward to spending time with her.

Becky and I had a good time getting acquainted. She was excited about the Christmas Coffees and felt we should give the women an opportunity to receive Christ, as originally planned. "We'll pray that the Spirit of God will work in Pam's mother's heart," I said. "By the way, Pam told me that her mom's bringing a friend with her.

She said both of them will walk out if they don't like the message. I mentioned the problem to the pastor. He suggested we seat the two women near the door. 'If they're not happy with the program they can slip out, but I really think they're just bluffing,' he said."

Becky and I spent some time in prayer and reassured each other that we were pleasing God in our endeavors.

The morning of the Coffee at Pam's house, I arrived with a sense of peace, remembering the words of my former pastor, Joe Stowell: "If we do the possible, God will do the impossible." I had experienced that many times and knew I had nothing to fear.

Besides Pam, Becky, and myself, four other women came. Pam's mom, Jean, and her friend Lou were delightful. We had a good time talking as we sipped our coffee. They didn't seem at all intimidated. Pam was the one who seemed nervous.

Finally we were asked to come into the living room and Pam introduced me: "Nellie will give us a brief message. It will be a good preparation for the holidays."

This was what I said:

> Christmas is the time of year when there seems to be unity in the community. [The women nodded and smiled.] There's an excitement and joy in the air as we talk to our neighbors about our plans for the holidays. But in the busyness of the season, it's easy to forget the real meaning of Christmas.
>
> I'm reminded of the time we spent Christmas in Florida. When I went to a department store to do some shopping, I noticed a sign in the window that said, "Shopping at———is the real meaning of Christmas." I couldn't believe it. *Does Christmas only mean spending a few dollars on gifts?* I thought.

I walked into the store and politely asked one of the saleswomen to call the manager so I might speak to him. He appeared concerned and asked whether something was wrong.

"Definitely," I answered. "I'm greatly offended by the sign in your window. The real meaning of Christmas is *not* shopping at your store. Jesus Christ is what Christmas is all about. He was born to die so that he might save us from our sins. It really hurts me to see your sign."

"I agree with you," he said. "We both know the real meaning of Christmas. But my boss told me to put the sign in the window."

"I would appreciate it if you would give your boss a message from me," I said kindly. "Tell him if he doesn't remove the sign, I will try to influence my friends not to shop at your store. I might also sue him for false advertising."

That kind of commercialism has crept in and blurred the reason we celebrate Christ's birthday. There was a time when I, too, looked forward to Christmas mainly because of the gifts I would receive. But now that I've made Jesus Christ Lord of my life, I anticipate the season with a new appreciation and awe. God gave us his Son, the best gift of all.

I'm overwhelmed when I think that Jesus Christ, who knew no sin, took the burden of my sin upon himself. He opted to be my substitute. I deserved to die, but he took my place. I have received God's gift of salvation by confessing my sin and acknowledging Jesus as my Savior. The greatest sin anyone can commit is to reject Jesus Christ. He is God's only provision for our sin.

There are usually people in a gathering such as this who have never received Jesus Christ as their Savior. I would like to give you an opportunity to do that today. If you would like to receive Christ, I will pray out loud and you can pray silently after me. It isn't so much the

words you say that are important to God, but the attitude of your heart.

At that point Pam left the room. I knew she was still
struggling, afraid that her mother and her friend would
leave.

Then I began to pray: "Dear heavenly Father, I thank
you for sending your Son, Jesus Christ, to die on the
cross for me. I confess I have sinned and gone my own
independent way. I now receive Jesus Christ as my Savior and Lord. Thank you for accepting me into your
family. Guide me and direct me in your way. In Jesus'
name I pray. Amen."

I gave all the women a piece of paper, asking each to
write her name on it. "This is the first time we've had a
Christmas Coffee," I said. "I'd appreciate it if you would
let us know if you enjoyed it and would like to do it
again. If you prayed to receive Christ, please put a check
mark by your name. When I see that, I will pray for you."

Three of the four guests put a check mark by their
name. The note from Pam's mom was a thank-you for
delivering God's message. Her friend Lou said the message was especially important to her this Christmas.
The third came from Mary Lou, who wrote: "My son
has received Christ. Even though he has had great sor-
row in his life, he finds God's strength sufficient. I want
that kind of faith. Thank you for taking time to talk to
us today. I received Jesus Christ today."

The fourth woman, Christine, got up to leave. She
seemed to be in a hurry. When she got to the door, she
turned and said, "You sounded so serious when you
spoke."

"Yes, our relationship to Christ is serious business," I
replied.

"I'll talk to you about it—sometime," she said.

Just then, Pam came out of the kitchen to say good-bye to Christine as she hurried out the door. After she left I asked Pam, "What happened to you? Are you all right?"

"I had butterflies in my stomach," she said. "I was so nervous about my mother and her friend, I actually got sick. But I want you to know that I did pray while you were talking. I desperately wanted my mom to accept Christ. I'm really surprised that she and her friend stayed."

"Pam, both your mom and Lou prayed to receive Christ today. Your fears were in vain. Isn't God good?"

"I can't believe it. I just can't believe it!" she exclaimed. "The whole neighborhood could have been here and I wouldn't have been nervous. It's just that my mother. . . ."

"I know," I said. "It's normal to become fearful over what someone close to you may do. It's also a time of testing—a time to hand over our fears to the Lord and put our trust in him."

Before Pam's mom left she said, "Nellie, would you be willing to have lunch with us after the holidays? It would be nice if you could tell us more about the Bible."

Of course I said, "I'd love to."

Postscript

Fear saps us of our energy and is never productive. It also robs us of our peace. But Jesus said, "Peace I leave with you; my peace I give you. I do not give to you as the world gives. Do not let your hearts be troubled and do not be afraid" (John 14:27).

Pam is a different person today because she is learning that God is in control of all things. She has witnessed a miracle, a change of mind and heart in her mother. It's a beginning. Philippians 1:6 says, "Being confident of this, that he who began a good work in you will carry it on to completion until the day of Christ Jesus."

Christine left early and seemed uncomfortable with my message. I didn't know if I would ever see her again, but I knew that Pam and Becky would have contact with her.

The following week, Becky came to me and said, "Jessica, my six-year-old, spent the evening with Christine's daughter, Gabrielle. An interesting thing happened. Gabrielle read some Bible verses that her grandmother had written down before she died. Then she asked Jessica if she could explain how to become a Christian. Even though my daughter is only six, she knows the Lord and can explain the way of salvation. She simply told Gabrielle she would have to confess that she had sinned against God and then receive Jesus as her Savior.

"'I'd like to do that,' Gabrielle said. Then Jessica prayed and helped her eight-year-old friend pray to receive Christ. At that point the bedroom door opened and Christine asked, 'What are you girls doing?'

"'We're reading verses from the Bible,' her daughter answered.

"'Oh,' she said as she closed the door."

The Christmas Coffees are over until next year. Only God knows the far-reaching results. Perhaps he will see to it that Christine opens the door to Jesus Christ.

*For God did not give us a spirit of timidity, but
a spirit of power, of love and of self-discipline.*

[2 Timothy 1:7]

13

Stepping Out in Faith

We're having our final preparation meeting for the Christmas Coffees next Wednesday," Lauren reminded me. "Most of the women are not experienced in public speaking. Some are very nervous about addressing a group, so we want a few people to listen to what they plan to say. This rehearsal will give them more confidence when the actual time comes, and they need our encouragement and prayers over this wonderful opportunity to speak out for the Lord."

"I'm really excited about what's happening in our church," I said to Lauren. "We've never done anything quite like this before. I'll plan to be in church early on Wednesday."

"You need to know that it's not only the speakers who are nervous; the hostesses are, too," Lauren said. "Some have never shared the gospel with their neighbors and are concerned about their response. It's understandable that they're a bit timid about this new venture."

"Well," I said, "this will be a good time to let the people next door or down the street know we are believers. I'll do all I can to encourage the speakers. I think this is a great evangelistic outreach. I can hardly wait to see what happens. If the women are willing to step out in faith, I know God will bless the results. After all, we're doing what Jesus commanded us to do when he told us to be his witnesses."

When I arrived at the meeting the following Wednesday, there was an air of excitement. The women seemed committed to the task even though unsure of themselves.

It was interesting to see different age groups represented. Even a few men were present, for they were going to speak to couples' groups, which would be held in the evening. There were sixty-five Christmas Coffees scheduled. Since this would be a first, everyone wanted the endeavor to be successful, a fruitful way to honor Jesus Christ.

"Nellie, I'd like you to listen to Karen Melby's message," Lauren said. "If you have any suggestions, feel free to tell her."

I was delighted, for I have a special interest in Karen. She is my daughter's namesake and was born the night of *our* Karen's senior piano recital. Her mother is a good friend of mine and had hoped to attend, but instead her baby was born. Karen's father, Paul Johnson, was in the audience, however. He congratulated our daughter after the concert. "You've worked hard to accomplish what you did tonight. We're proud of you," he said. "We thought you'd like to know that we've decided to name our new baby after you, Karen."

Our daughter was greatly moved and later asked us why anyone would name a child after her.

My husband said, "Probably because of the discipline you've shown in your music. And perhaps because of your love for Christ. That's a good combination."

Over the years, I have watched my friends' daughter grow into a lovely young lady. I pray for Karen often and was keenly interested in hearing what she had prepared for the Christmas Coffees.

As Karen came toward me, she made a face and said, "I'm scared. You've got to pray for me."

"You, afraid?" I asked with a smile. "I thought you and Scott sponsored evangelistic dinners while living in Chicago after you married. Aren't you used to sharing the gospel with strangers by now?"

"But I wasn't the speaker," she said. "That's what makes me nervous. Please pray for me."

"I'll pray that God will give you peace and the confidence to do a good job for him. Now let's hear what you're planning to tell your group."

"I had a real struggle this week," Karen told me. "I felt so inadequate. I didn't even know how to get started. Finally I told the Lord how I felt and asked him to guide my thinking. As I was praying, the thoughts came to my mind. Now I'd like to read what I've prepared."

As I listened, Karen talked about the love displayed by her family, explaining that Christmas was always a special time of warmth and joy in their home. She told of a surprise gift her father brought out each year after everything else had been unwrapped. All the family members got a gift of money with which to buy anything they desired. No strings attached. He did this year after year—topping everything with a special dose of love.

Karen said, "I remember thinking, *Why does he do that? I don't deserve it. He must really love us a lot to be so generous.* "As time went on," she continued, "I realized that as great as my dad's gift was, it couldn't compare with the gift my heavenly Father has given us. God gave us his only begotten Son to die on the cross for our sins."

I continued to listen to Karen's message, which she presented very well. When she finished, I said, "Karen, you've given a clear gospel message. It isn't the great orators who win people to Christ. God uses those who are available and obedient to his Word. He has asked us to be his witnesses. Now we'll pray that God will prepare hearts to receive your message. I'll be praying, too, that God will quiet your fears and that joy will be your portion."

"I have no idea how many women will attend the Coffee," Karen said after we prayed, "but that's not important. I just want to do a good job for the Lord."

Before she left, Karen turned to me and said, "Now that Scott and I are back in Michigan, we want to continue to have an outreach. I do hope all goes well at the Coffees."

"You're taking a step of faith," I told her. "Remember what Jesus said in Acts 1:8: 'But you will receive power when the Holy Spirit comes on you; and you will be my witnesses in Jerusalem, and in all Judea and Samaria, and to the ends of the earth.' Birmingham is your Jerusalem right now, so you're all set. By obeying Jesus' commands, you not only please him but will experience joy the unbelieving world can neither have nor understand. We'll just wait and see what happens."

The week of the Christmas Coffees finally came, and the response to the message of salvation was far above our expectations. The Holy Spirit had prepared the hearts of those who attended.

When I called Karen to see how she got along, she said excitedly, "I can't believe what happened. I just can't believe it."

"Tell me about it. Your meetings must have gone well. How did the women respond to your message?"

"Nine women came to the first meeting. Eight of them indicated on a slip of paper that they had prayed with me to receive Christ."

"What about your second group?" I asked.

"Seven women came, and six said they'd be interested in having a Bible study. I'm overwhelmed. It's hard to believe God could use me in this way."

"Karen, it's been said before, over and over again: 'If we do the possible, God will do the impossible.'"

Postscript

The door of opportunity was opened, and God's available servant walked through. When a step of growth was taken by Karen, the result was joy and a blessing from God upon his servant.

Karen realized that on her own she could do nothing. When she sought God's guidance and leaned on him for understanding, her mind was activated. The Holy Spirit opened her mind to God's thoughts and gave her the courage to step out in faith and boldly speak the Good News.

> Trust in the LORD with all your heart
>   and lean not on your own understanding;
> in all your ways acknowledge him,
>   and he will make your paths straight. [Prov. 3:5–6]

We have different gifts, according to the grace given us. If a man's gift is prophesying, let him use it in proportion to his faith. If it is serving, let him serve; if it is teaching, let him teach; if it is encouraging, let him encourage; if it is contributing to the needs of others, let him give generously; if it is leadership, let him govern diligently; if it is showing mercy, let him do it cheerfully.

[Romans 12:6–8]

14

Teamwork

A woman in one of my seminars raised her hand and said, "I love the Lord and I know he's given me the gift of hospitality. I'd like to have a Bible study in my home, but I don't have the ability to instruct a group in the Scriptures."

"Why don't you find someone who has the gift of teaching and combine your gifts?" I said. "And perhaps you have another Christian friend who has the gift of organization and might be willing to help you get started. God has given every believer a gift for the purpose of edifying the church. We all need each other, because no one person has all the gifts. Many things can be accomplished for the Lord if we don't try to do it all by ourselves. It must be a team effort."

Then I told the group about Kathy, a good friend of mine:

> Kathy approached me at church one Sunday morning and said, "My husband and I are hosting an evangelistic dinner. I've invited my Christian friends, but I told them each to bring another couple. I said, 'We want you to bring unbelievers, because this is to be an opportunity for outreach.'"
>
> When I commented to Kathy that it sounded like a great idea, she said, "We'd like *you* to be the speaker. Will you consider it and check your calendar to see if May 29th is open?"
>
> I called Kathy that evening and told her I was free to speak. "I'd love to be a part of your effort to reach people for Christ," I said. "I'm so happy you're doing this. I'll pray with you that the Holy Spirit will have freedom to work in hearts."
>
> Kathy's husband, Ben, had the gift of teaching. They held a weekly Bible study in their home, and the people who attended were among those invited to the dinner.

> My friend's gift of hospitality definitely set the stage for a successful evening. Thirty-five people came. When we arrived, there were no lights on in the living room or dining area. It must have seemed strange to the guests! Kathy smiled and whispered in my ear, "I want everyone to be surprised—but not until later."
>
> We were all ushered downstairs to the family room for hors d'oeuvres and a time of getting acquainted. Then we were asked to come upstairs and the lights were turned on. Everyone began talking at once. "Oh,

it's beautiful! Absolutely beautiful," we all said. Ecru-colored lace tablecloths with peach underskirts were placed on round tables, each with candles and a bouquet of flowers in the center. Kathy had done her very best to make the setting attractive. It was a lot of work, but she did it to honor the Lord. The dinner was delicious. Friends with the gift of helping had brought the desserts—seven in all and each one different.

If a friendly dinner was all Kathy had hoped to accomplish, it would have been a success. But she wanted more. Her chief desire was to have her guests hear the gospel. That's where I came in.

After the guests had finished dessert, I was introduced as the speaker, and they arranged their chairs to face me. Since they had come prepared to hear a Bible message, this was not a surprise.

I shared with them that although I had gone to church and heard about Christ for many years, one day I realized there must be more to Christianity than church attendance. I told them reading a portion of the Bible every night had become a meaningless ritual for me. "My mind would wander," I said, "and I couldn't remember what I had read. Then our pastor reminded us one Sunday that reading the Bible wasn't enough. We had to obey it.

"That helped me realize that Jesus Christ died for my sins," I continued. "He took my place—he opted to be my substitute. He came to seek and to save the lost. I knew I was a lost sinner. Even if my good deeds outweighed my bad ones, it wouldn't be enough. God demanded perfection, but I couldn't meet his standards. Only Jesus Christ could do that. I confessed that I was a sinner and accepted God's provision for me by asking Jesus Christ to be my Savior and Lord.

"A woman said to me once, 'I'll take my chances. I know God will accept me on the basis of all the good things I've done. In fact, I've been honored by my church for my many good deeds.'

"I reminded her of Ephesians 2:8–9, which says, 'For it is by grace you have been saved, through faith—and this not from yourselves, it is the gift of God—not by works, so that no one can boast.'

"'I'll take my chances,' she repeated. There was nothing more I could say."

I then turned to the audience at Kathy's house and said, "Each one of you has to choose the path you want to take. Tonight you have an opportunity to make it known." I asked those who desired to accept Christ as Savior to put a check mark on their name tag. Six people responded. Among them was a Muslim psychiatrist who had attended Ben's Bible class for several weeks. Because the Spirit of God had been working in his heart and prepared him for this moment, he made a decision to follow Christ. When the meeting was over, the man came to me and said, "I accepted Jesus Christ as my Savior tonight. I can see the difference Jesus makes in a person's life. Christians have a joy that Muslims don't have."

After I finished telling my seminar about Kathy and Ben's evangelistic dinner, I said, "You see, Jesus *does* make all the difference in the world. He makes life worth living. And each of us can experience the joy of presenting the gospel to others if we combine our own spiritual gifts with those of other believers. We can truly honor the Lord if we all work together as a team."

Postscript

Kathy and Ben are continuing to serve the Lord faithfully. Both of them draw on their friends for help, for they have learned the principle of teamwork.

"I heard you participated in the Christmas Coffees the church sponsored," I remarked to Kathy one day.

"Actually," she said, "we decided to have a luncheon instead. We held it at Ben's office and invited all the secretaries in the building. It was the most exciting thing we've ever done for the Lord."

That's quite an undertaking, I thought. I knew Ben was an attorney. "How could you use his office?" I asked. "What if his clients walked in?"

"Oh, that wouldn't have mattered," she said. "He has a suite of offices. We met in his library."

"How many floors and offices are there in Ben's building?" I asked. "And who gave the message?"

"There are twenty-five floors and fifty offices. Betty was the speaker. She had recently said to me, 'I used to teach a Bible class and be active in Christian work. But all I do now is sell real estate.' She seemed disappointed in herself, so I suggested she give the Christmas message at our luncheon. She seemed a little hesitant, but I convinced her to accept the challenge. Betty did a beautiful job—and thirty-seven women came to the luncheon."

When I asked Kathy how she managed all the work involved, she said excitedly, "I couldn't believe the help my friends offered. One woman wanted to help serve. Another woman did the decorating. Others brought desserts."

"How did the guests respond?" I asked.

"Well, six women marked on their name tags that they had received Christ. Ten indicated they would like a weekly Bible study. We've already started that. Everyone brings a bag lunch and I serve the beverages."

"That's absolutely terrific," I exclaimed.

"That's not all. We told them that each office will

receive a gift in January and another one in February. We've already given them 'Walk Through the Bible' for the month of January.

"One of the other secretaries heard about the Bible study and called to ask what was going on. When I explained, she asked whether she could come and bring a friend. 'Absolutely,' I answered."

"How do you account for the enthusiastic response?" I asked Kathy.

"I believe the recent war with Iraq and the state of the economy have frightened people. They are looking for answers and are turning to God. We have an opportunity of a lifetime. I know, Nellie, that God has given every Christian a job to do."

Kathy and so many others like her are daily showing the truth of God's Word that "there are different kinds of gifts, but the same Spirit. There are different kinds of service, but the same Lord. There are different kinds of working, but the same God works all of them in all men" (1 Cor. 12:4–6).

And we know that in all things God works for the good of those who love him, who have been called according to his purpose.

[Romans 8:28]

15

Tragedy or Blessing?

I've seen that young woman sitting near the front of the church for the past few Sundays," I said to Paul. "She's absolutely radiant. What a beautiful smile! But look at her—she has lost her leg four inches below the knee. How can she be so happy?"

"Why don't you get acquainted with her?" my husband suggested. "Go and talk to her after the service."

"I plan to do just that. She fascinates me."

After I introduced myself and the woman told me her name was Lisa, I asked, "Do you mind telling me about your leg?"

"Not at all," Lisa said.

"I was run over by a train. I was in Germany at the time. But," she added with a smile, "in two weeks I'm getting a new leg. I can hardly wait."

Lisa began to attend Wednesday-evening prayer meetings regularly. We often sat behind her and chatted before the service began.

It was a happy day when Lisa came to church with her new prosthesis. She grinned from ear to ear and said, "See, I'm just like new! The ankle looks too large now but will look better in a few weeks. The doctor will get it down to proper size by wrapping it tightly with foam. It will gradually take shape and look more like a normal ankle."

"How long have you been a Christian?" I asked her.

"About seven months," she told me. "It's quite a story. I'll tell you about it some time." I suggested having lunch together the following week, and we agreed that Tuesday was convenient for both of us.

I was excited when the doorbell rang on Tuesday. I knew I would enjoy getting to know this enthusiastic young lady, who told me she was thirty and the oldest of her parents' offspring. After we finished lunch, we sat in the living room and I asked Lisa one question after another about herself.

"Do you come from a family of believers?" I asked.

"Not really. My sister Jackie came to Christ eight years ago, after attending a retreat at a Presbyterian church. She was really turned on for the Lord and immediately started in on the family, especially me. She tried to convince me that the only way to God was through Jesus Christ. I didn't want to hear it, but she wouldn't give up. We almost came to blows about it. Because Jackie loved our family and knew she had the truth, she'd say over and over again, 'You've *got* to listen.' But I kept resisting."

"Did you have any religious beliefs?" I asked.

"I was fascinated by Eastern philosophy, spiritism, and all sorts of strange ideas. Once, a group of us was invited to a friend's house. There I met an evil-looking man who frightened me. He came up close to me and whispered, 'Hand over your life to me and everything will be wonderful.' I felt as though Satan was speaking to me. It was so weird that I ran out of the room. I knew something was wrong and wanted to put my hands over my ears. Soon after that, I began remembering my grandmother's prayers. She was a believer and prayed for all of us."

"Was she the only Christian in your family in those days?" I asked.

"Yes, and the picture of her praying had stayed with me, even though I tried to block it out. When my sister began praying for me, too, I felt as though a warfare was going on inside of me."

"That's exactly what happens," I commented.

"Then I met a young Christian at my cousin's house," Lisa continued. "His name was Kevin. I told him I had a hard time believing in such miracles as the virgin birth. I asked him, 'Why can't I believe in Jesus? I believe in all the evil things, but I just can't seem to believe in God.' He challenged me to read the Scriptures and gave me Josh McDowell's book *Evidence That Demands a Verdict*. As he handed me the book, I told him that I didn't believe the Bible.

"'Read this,' he said. 'Then we'll talk again.' After reading the book, I was convinced that Jesus was who he claimed to be. I even told God I believed in him and his Son. I thought I now had faith in God. But I believed in my head, not in my heart. I hadn't made him Lord of my life. I still wanted to be in charge. One day I told the Lord, 'If you see anything in my life that needs changing, work on me. Change me—that is if you think it's necessary.' I thought if it was important to God, he'd change me without any help from me. And if he was really God, he'd do a good job.

"I continued to smoke and drink. I lied and cheated and was a rebellious creature. Even though I knew I was disobeying God, I expected the Lord to change me without my cooperation. I was attending Wayne State University at the time, majoring in economics and getting all A's. People told me I was a good student and a wonderful person. But on the inside I was miserable.

"I remember once being very drunk while driving. When I came to myself, I prayed, 'Lord, please don't let me kill anyone when I'm drunk.' But I kept on drinking.

"Last year I went to Europe with a friend and had a ball. We went to Greece, Italy, Belgium, and Holland. We talked to many people and saw all the sights. We were in Munich, Germany, when the accident happened. I stepped off the subway, lost my balance, and fell between the third and fourth cars. Before they were able to get me free, the train started up again. One car ran over my leg.

"When I woke up in the hospital, I thought, *God must really love me. He let me live.* I knew that lots of people were praying for me. God hadn't given up on me!

"My sister flew over from the States to be by my side, not yet knowing that God had answered her prayers. When I awoke and saw Jackie by my bed, I said, 'Isn't this wonderful?'

"'What do you mean?' she asked.

"'It's a miracle. This accident—it's God's doing. Now he's saved both of us.' We laughed and cried together. She knew, along with me, that it had to be this way.

God had to do something drastic to get my attention. Actually, I had asked for it.

"The doctor told me I had a thirty-percent chance of survival. I had no problem with that, because I finally understood that God loved me. I was content. Now my greatest desire in life is to share God's love with those who don't know my Savior. How else can I say thanks for what he has done for me? I've never been happier in my life, but I'm so sorry for the wasted years."

As Lisa left, I noticed how well she walked. "No one would ever know you had an artificial limb," I said.

"And I'm expecting to run in no time at all," she said cheerfully, waving as she said, "Good-bye. And thanks for listening."

Postscript

Lisa continues to be an inspiration to many people as she grows in the Lord and witnesses to others. She has good friends who are a great support to her. They are part of her new family—the family of God.

"I wouldn't have missed this experience for anything," Lisa told me recently. "My accident was the reason I really got acquainted with God."

When Lisa related her story to me, I was reminded of Psalm 139:1–7, 23–24:

> O LORD, you have searched me
>   and you know me.
> You know when I sit and when I rise;
>   you perceive my thoughts from afar.
> You discern my going out and my lying down;
>   you are familiar with all my ways.
> Before a word is on my tongue
>   you know it completely, O LORD.

You hem me in—behind and before;
    you have laid your hand upon me.
Such knowledge is too wonderful for me,
    too lofty for me to attain.
Where can I go from your Spirit?
    Where can I flee from your presence? . . .
Search me, O God, and know my heart;
    test me and know my anxious thoughts.
See if there is any offensive way in me,
    and lead me in the way everlasting.

Be very careful, then, how you live—not as unwise but as wise, making the most of every opportunity, because the days are evil.

[Ephesians 5:15–16]

16

Just What the Doctor Ordered

I want you to take this pill," the doctor said.

"What is it?" I asked.

"You don't need to know, I just want you to take it," he answered. His back was turned to me, so I couldn't see what he was doing. I thought he was writing a prescription.

"I'm sorry, Doctor Proctor, but I never take any medication without knowing what it is. I'm allergic to some medicines, you know. Why won't you tell me what it is?" I persisted.

"Be patient. I'll give it to you in a minute."

"Well, you may give it to me, but I won't swallow it until you tell me what it is," I repeated.

He turned toward me and gave me a strange look. Then he handed me a tiny booklet. "Look at this," he said. A sticker with his name was printed on one side. "That's what I want you to take."

I was still puzzled.

"Turn it over," he said.

On the back was printed: "Today's GOS-PILL . . . Very good for the heart."

"I should have known," I said. "You're such a big tease."

"I have several booklets I give away. The one I give depends on the person. I need to know where he or she is coming from. I try to be sensitive to my patients' needs."

My doctor knows I'm a believer, and we've had many good talks together. He was just having some fun.

I opened the booklet. The first page said, "Prescribed by Dr. Conrad" (his first name). The following pages had wonderful Scripture verses. The gospel was outlined in a clear way.

"It's my way of sharing the Word of God," he said as he left the room to attend to another patient. Gina, his nurse, stayed with me to give me a treatment to clear my sinuses.

"Do you attend the same church as Doctor Proctor?" I asked. "I know many of his nurses do."

"No, I don't attend church at all."

"That's too bad," I said. "Maybe we could talk about it."

"I don't need that," she said. She seemed cool and aloof.

Oh, oh, I thought, *I'm being pushy. I should have been more sensitive.* "I'm sorry if I've offended you," I said.

"I'm always concerned when people are not interested in learning more about God."

"You didn't offend me. It's just that everyone gets on my back about going to church. The same thing happened at the last place I worked. Something good came out of it, though," she said. "When I left, they gave me a reference Bible. I read it all the time. I know I'm a Christian. I've accepted Christ as my Savior, but I've had some bad experiences in church. That's why I don't care to attend.

"I visited one local church to observe what went on," she continued. "I was treated very coolly because I wasn't one of them. At least that's what I thought. I didn't feel comfortable."

"Gina, the Bible says, 'Let us not give up meeting together, as some are in the habit of doing, but let us encourage one another' [Heb. 10:25b]. As believers, we're supposed to be witnesses for Jesus Christ. If you talked to someone about the Lord and he or she asked, 'Where do you attend church?' would you feel comfortable saying, 'I don't attend church, I just read my Bible'?"

"Well, I don't do much witnessing," she said. "I really don't know how."

I reached in my bag and gave her a copy of my book *What Do You Say When?* "Maybe this will give you some ideas," I said.

"Oh, thank you," she said and came over to give me a hug. "I will treasure this and I'm sure it will help me."

"I'd love to have you visit our church, Gina. We have a large number of young people about your age. They are a lively group and seem to have a love for people. You probably need to be encouraged in the Christian walk. Would you care to come with us to church on

Easter, two weeks from Sunday? We'll take you out to dinner after the service."

"Let me check it out with my parents, Mrs. Pickard. They go to an evangelical church. Maybe I should try their church first. I'll get back to you in a couple of days."

When Gina called back she said, "I've decided to attend Easter services with my folks. Some other relatives will be there, too. I'm really getting excited about going. I'll let you know how it works out."

"I'm glad you've decided to be with God's people. If you ever want to visit with us, my offer still stands."

Postscript

I have sent several of my friends to see Dr. Proctor. Besides being a good ear, nose, and throat specialist, he has a great sense of humor. He also has a unique way of sharing his faith. Who would refuse a doctor's prescription, especially one as important as the GOS-PILL?

There are many ways and methods of witnessing. Our great Creator endows us with fresh ideas every day. There's no need to lie awake at night, wondering what we will say. The Spirit of God puts the right words in our minds as we need them.

All believers need Christian fellowship. We must encourage each other. Although Gina is a believer, she will grow by hearing the Word of God expounded, especially in the company of believers in her own age group. Discussing the Scriptures and learning Christian principles will strengthen her walk with God.

I'm looking forward to seeing Gina again. I thank God for giving me a chance to talk with this lovely young lady, so I could share what he says about Christians' assembling together.

"Let the word of Christ dwell in you richly as you teach and admonish one another with all wisdom, and as you sing psalms, hymns and spiritual songs with gratitude in your hearts to God" (Col. 3:16).

Preach the Word; be prepared in season and out of season; correct, rebuke and encourage—with great patience and careful instruction.

[2 Timothy 4:2]

17

Seizing the Moment

I have always regretted that I couldn't go with my husband to Hershey, Pennsylvania, on a business trip he once took with one of the officers of his company. He came home with glowing reports of that fair city, but all I was interested in was the chocolate. "Did they give you samples to take home to your family?" I asked.

"Not to take home," he said as he patted my shoulder. "I'll have to take you there sometime." That was many years ago and we still haven't visited Hershey together.

I was recently reminded of my husband's trip when my friend Phil Buckingham told me about an interesting experience he had with the cashier at the candy counter of a drugstore.

"Ever since I visited the candy factory in Hershey, Pennsylvania," he had said to the clerk, "I've had a yen for these chocolate kisses. It seemed to me the whole town smelled like chocolate. The aroma was wonderful. I noticed that even the tops of the light posts were shaped like a Hershey Kiss. Some posts were wrapped in silver and the others were a brown chocolate color. When I went to bed that night I think I must have fallen asleep the minute my head touched the pillow."

"You must have been in seventh heaven," the cashier replied.

"Seventh heaven? Well, I'm not dead yet. But I know that when I do die, I'm going to heaven. What about you?" Phil asked her.

The cashier was taken aback for a minute. Then she said, "I'm not sure, but I certainly hope so."

"Tell me," Phil said, "if you were to die today and God said to you, 'Why should I let you into heaven?' what would you say?"

"I'd tell God all the good things I've done."

"In other words, you're depending on yourself to get to heaven. That's too bad, because the Bible says you don't get to heaven by your good works."

"How else then?" the cashier asked.

Phil said, "First let me tell you what the Bible says about working your way to heaven: 'For it is by grace you have been saved, through faith—and this not from yourselves, it is the gift of God—not by works. . . .' That's from Ephesians 2:8–9. It means that only by confessing to God you're a sinner, and receiving Jesus Christ as your Savior, will you be accepted into the family of God."

"I'll have to think about that," the cashier told Phil as she gave him his change.

Phil said all he could at the time. The rest is up to the Spirit of God. Perhaps God will send someone else to water the seed that was sown that day because Phil was alert to his circumstances and spoke up for the Lord.

My friend Olga works in the designer room at one of the leading department stores in our area. I have heard that she is one of the top salespersons in her company. She, like Phil, loves the Lord and speaks up whenever she has the opportunity. The week before Easter, one of her co-workers said to her, "This is the first year in centuries that everything falls into place on the calendar. Passover, Good Friday, and Easter all come in the correct chronological order."

"We have services at our church on Good Friday," Olga said, "and I'd like to attend. But I have to work. That is a very important day for me, because it is the day Jesus Christ died on the cross for my sins."

"A lot of Jews in those days were crucified," her co-worker commented.

"But Jesus rose from the dead. That's why Christians celebrate Easter. It means that we, too, can have eternal life."

"That's a myth," the other woman said with a sneer. "You don't believe that stuff do you?"

"According to God's Word, the Bible, it is absolutely true. I know that God sent his only Son to die for my sins. He took my place on the cross. I accept that by faith."

Olga has told me that she talks to many people about the Lord. I know she is discreet and sensitive as to how far she can go. She also has the gift of encouragement. Many times she will personally deliver an outfit to her customers to help them out. Both her words and her actions are a positive testimony for Christ.

I thought Fred, another friend of mine, had a good idea about witnessing to his relatives. He phoned one day and said, "Nellie, I'm not good with words. I wonder if you'd be willing to help me out."

"I'll do what I can. What do you have in mind?" I asked.

"Well, ever since the seizure that almost took my life, I've realized that our time on earth is so very short. I'm concerned about my relatives. I need to share the gospel with them."

"Do they live in this area?" I asked.

"No, they don't, but there's a perfect opportunity coming up. We're going to have a family reunion in July. About fifty people will be coming from all over. I'd like to write a letter to my relatives before they arrive, telling how they can know for sure if they're going to heaven."

When Fred asked for some ideas, I suggested some Bible verses, then helped him draft a letter. I thought this was a unique way to witness, and Fred's concern for his relatives was touching. He gave me permission to reprint his letter:

> Dear —
>
> I am excited when I think of meeting fifty or sixty of my relatives at our family reunion. That doesn't happen too often in a lifetime. It certainly will be a special time.
>
> The older I get, the more I think about another reunion—with those who have received Jesus Christ as their Savior.
>
> My concern lately has been this: Will all the ones who attend the first reunion be at the second one? Since I've

lost touch with so many of you throughout the years, I really don't know.

I feel I have an obligation to those of you who don't know "The Way" to tell you what Jesus Christ said in John 14:6: "I am the way and the truth and the life. No one comes to the Father except through me."

I'm enclosing some verses from the Bible that plainly show how you, too, can know Jesus as your personal Savior. If you already know my Savior, then these verses will cause you to give thanks for your salvation.

Man is sinful—Romans 3:23

Sin has a penalty—Romans 6:23

Christ paid the penalty—Romans 5:8

Salvation is a free gift—Ephesians 2:8–9

Christ is our salvation—John 10:9

We must receive him—John 1:12

You have to pay the fare for the first reunion, but if you know Jesus Christ as your Savior, your final reunion will be free. Christ paid for your ticket by the blood he shed for you on the cross. Just think, we can enter scot-free.

I send this letter with my love and concern—please take it in that spirit.

In Christ's love,

Fred and Melba

After we had finished working on Fred's letter, he said, "Please pray with me, Nellie, that my relatives will realize that life is short. Pray that any who are not yet believers will respond positively to my letter and that they won't put off the decision to receive Christ as their Savior any longer."

Postscript

Sometimes a person will ask a question or make a statement that opens up the possibility of witnessing for the Lord.

Whoever would think of chocolate candy in that way? Phil wasn't thinking about sharing his faith when he told the clerk he had visited the town where Hershey's candy was made. But, as soon as the word *heaven* was mentioned, he was aware of the opportunity to talk about being prepared. He then took the conversation as far as seemed prudent.

Olga picked up on the woman talking about the upcoming holidays. Because Good Friday was important to her, that's how she contributed to the conversation. She wasn't timid about saying she accepted Christ's death and resurrection by faith. She believed the Scriptures and said so.

Fred had a concern for his relatives and wanted them to know he cared. He also wanted to be sure they knew the way to God. *Life is short,* he thought. *I must help them redeem the time.*

People are looking for answers to important questions. Many are wise about the ways of the world but ignorant when it comes to God and his eternal truths. The Lord expects us to be bold in his service—to seize every possible moment to speak in Jesus' name.

Fred was called home to be with the Lord before his letter was in the mail. He had made arrangements, and the letters will go out with copies of this book.

If we confess our sins, he is faithful and just and will forgive us our sins and purify us from all unrighteousness.

[1 John 1:9]

18

Healed in Prison

As Ed was finishing out the last few days of his prison sentence, his heart was full of praise and thanksgiving to God. Though keenly aware of the arthritic pain in his back, he looked at his steel cot and thin mattress and prayed, "Thank you, Lord, that I wasn't made to sleep on the floor." When he looked through the iron bars on his cell window, he was filled with the wonder of God's creation. Later he told us the rest of his prayer:

Thank you, Lord, for the birds and flowers, the trees, the sky, and water. You've given them all for us to enjoy. I never want to take your works for granted again. And, Lord, I didn't think I could ever say this to you, but thank you for allowing me to go to prison. You had to

hit me hard, but you got my attention. You have taught
me about priorities, so the rest of my life is yours. You
will be first, my family second, and business third.
Thank you for forgiving me. I will always want and need
your guidance.

Ed was far from a hardened criminal. He was a high-
ly skilled sales-and-marketing expert who had received
many awards. Ed had lectured at Michigan State and
Cornell and been invited to the White House to represent the hotel industry. For fifteen years, he was vice-
president of sales and marketing at a posh thousand-
room hotel and club in Florida. Under his tenure at the
resort, sales rose tenfold. By the world's standards, Ed
lived extremely well. Most people would say, "He had
it made." So how did Ed land in prison—this man who
at one point in his life mortgaged his home to help
build a church?

My husband and I had occasion to have lunch with
Ed and his wife, Jeanne, whom we knew as members of
the church we attended in Florida. Since we were just
winter visitors, we had not read any of the newspaper
articles connected with his incarceration. "Tell me, Ed,"
I asked, "why were you in prison?"

"I unwisely got involved in a kickback scheme," he
said ruefully. "An associate of mine for over thirty years,
a man I trusted, came up with the idea. Although I said
no at the beginning, later he told me there would be
ten other participants and convinced me there was
nothing wrong."

"Being a Christian, didn't that bother you?" I asked.

"You bet it did, but this happened at a time when I
had taken my eyes off the Lord. That's a dangerous sit-

uation! I understand now what Peter was talking about when he said, 'Your enemy the devil prowls around like a roaring lion looking for someone to devour' [1 Peter 5:8b]. It's the weak Christian the devil is looking for. That was me. It didn't seem so bad at first. I was busy working and making money. But, even though I wasn't close to the Lord at the time, God never left me. The Holy Spirit kept after me, convicting me that I should come clean. Soon I was miserable with guilt.

"What did you do about it?" I asked.

"Since I knew the day would come when I would have to pay everything back, I didn't touch the money except to put it in a special fund. But I became a recluse. I was depressed and ashamed and didn't want to speak to people at church. When I came home I went to my room and pulled the shades. Since my guilt was more than I could bear, my health began to fail."

"Did Jeanne notice your change?" I asked.

"Oh, I knew she was concerned about me. She asked a lot of questions about why I was so glum and wanted to know what was wrong. I kept telling her I was just tired.

"Finally I couldn't keep it to myself any longer. 'I have defrauded my customers,' I told Jeanne. 'I have sinned against God, and I've let you down. I want to make restitution. Can you find it in your heart to forgive me and help me make things right?'"

"Were you able to forgive Ed right away?" I asked Jeanne.

"I was angry and hurt, of course. Then Ed got angry because I was angry, so I said, 'Now wait a minute. How do you expect me to react? Give me a minute to catch my breath.' When I realized the load of guilt he'd been carrying, it explained everything. I put my arms around him and assured him of my love. I told him, 'I'll stick with you no matter what. With God's help we'll work it out.'"

Ed, with tears in his eyes, turned to me and said, "I was overwhelmed with Jeanne's love and forgiveness. I couldn't have made it without her support."

"Perhaps this is what our wedding vows mean when we promise to stay together for better or for worse," I said. "But what about your children? Did you tell them right away?"

"The thought of telling them was agony," Ed said, "but I knew it had to be done, even though I might lose their love and respect. I had to give myself up to the authorities and I didn't want the children to hear it from anyone else. Of course they were shocked. But they put their arms around me and said, 'Dad, we love you. We'll pray for you and support you through this.'

"Next I went to my pastor and told him I had a problem. He could tell I was distraught but I was too ashamed to tell him the complete story."

"Then what did you do?" I asked.

"I went to my lawyer, who advised me not to turn myself in. 'It would be like waving a red flag,' he said. 'You haven't been accused yet and may never be.' I found another lawyer, who gave me the same advice. I was especially concerned about Jeanne and what would happen to her financially. But I was shocked when this lawyer suggested that we divide our joint property and then get a divorce. 'That way they can't touch her money, and you can always remarry later,' he said.

"At Jeanne's urging, we went to a third lawyer. He gave me the same advice as the other two. 'What about my conscience?' I asked. 'How do I correct my wrongs?

This whole thing goes against my Christian beliefs. What do I do with the money? I haven't spent a cent.'

"'This is a joke,' the lawyer laughed. 'You take the money, but you don't spend it. If it will alleviate some of your guilt, give *me* the money and I'll give it to charity.'

"I left his office heartsick. Even after seeing a Christian psychologist, I found no relief. The guilt was tearing me apart. I resigned my job, hoping that would settle matters.

"I finally decided to visit a longtime trusted minister who had once been a prison chaplain. After telling him my story, I asked whether he knew of a good lawyer who would agree that I should turn myself in and would represent me in court. Fortunately he did, and an appointment was set up immediately.

"This attorney was very kind. He said that because of my age and general background I would probably be put on probation or, at worst, under house arrest. He then made arrangements to see the prosecutor. At that point I decided to tell my pastor the whole story."

"What was his reaction?" I asked.

"He had had no idea of the reason for my distraught condition. I told him I had confessed my sin to God and planned to resign from the church office I held. Jeanne offered to resign from the women's ministries, too.

"Pastor said, 'There's no reason why Jeanne should resign. She hasn't done anything wrong.' He then said, 'God has forgiven you, and I forgive you.'

"'But,' I told him, 'I just can't forgive myself.'

"My pastor helped me understand that lack of self-forgiveness is pride, whereby we put ourselves above God. It reveals a failure to trust the One who has offered us unconditional love and forgiveness."

"Why were you eventually sent to prison?" I asked. "That wasn't what your lawyer expected."

"That was quite a surprise," Ed replied. "The prosecutor was not as sympathetic as my lawyer. He told me I could get anywhere from nine to seventeen years. The lawyer and prosecutor went back and forth. My lawyer argued that it was my first offense, but the prosecutor was determined that white-collar crime must stop and that I should be made the example. I was sentenced to two and a half years.

"Of course, I was shocked and depressed at the sentence. They took me to the county jail overnight, then to South Florida Reception Center. I thought I was on my way to a minimum-security prison, but I was placed in maximum security—with hardened criminals. I was there for two weeks. Then, because of my deep depression, I was temporarily put in the medical center for another two weeks.

"My stay in maximum security was a humiliating experience. I was stripped of any remaining dignity. At first my depression got worse and I didn't want to live. I had disappointed God, my family, and my church. I was a failure. One of the inmates had told me he could get me anything I wanted. Since I just wanted to die, I asked him if he could get me a pill so I could end it all.

"But God wouldn't let me do it. Suddenly a verse from the Bible flooded my mind. It was 1 Corinthians 6:19–20: 'Do you not know that your body is a temple of the Holy Spirit. . . ? You are not your own; you were bought at a price. Therefore honor God with your body.' I realized that suicide was no answer. All I could do was cast myself on God and plead for mercy."

"Did that give you relief?" I asked Ed.

"That was the beginning of the healing process. I began to devour Scripture. I read Psalm 51 over and over again. With David, who had also sinned greatly, I prayed, 'Have mercy on me, O God, according to your unfailing love; according to your great compassion blot out my transgressions. Wash away all my iniquity and cleanse me from my sin. . . . Against you, you only, have I sinned and done what is evil in your sight.'

"I knew my greatest sin was against God. He created me and formed me. Because I had received Jesus Christ as my Savior, knowing 1 John 1:9 was a comfort: 'If we confess our sins, he is faithful and just and will forgive us our sins and purify us from all unrighteousness.'"

"Ed, did you do anything constructive while in prison?" I asked.

"While in maximum security I was given a job as a clerk in the tool room. *This place needs some improving,* I thought. The prison authorities liked my ideas and I was able to use my business experience. I was allowed to redesign the tool room, develop a new job description, and compile an inventory. I got satisfaction out of being useful.

"After a few weeks I was moved to Dade Correctional Center, which was a minimum-security facility. That was a great improvement. I spent a lot of time in chapel and joined a Bible study group. Soon I began to witness to other inmates and share with them about God's love and forgiveness. When I saw that God could use me even in prison, I could praise him for this experience.

"One day I received over four hundred cards from the church. My pastor had encouraged the congregation to continue praying for me and to let me know they still cared. I was overwhelmed, and so were the prison officials. The chaplain announced the news at the service and read some of the cards. 'We are looking forward to your homecoming,' some said.

"Because of my good behavior, and prison overcrowding, my sentence was reduced to a little over five months. I finished my prison term on a Tuesday. Sunday morning I went to church with Jeanne and sat near the front. That wasn't easy. *How will I be received?* I wondered. But I prayed, 'Whatever happens, Lord, I'm going to serve you the rest of my life.'"

Paul and I were there in church that Sunday. After the opening hymn, the pastor said, "I want to tell you all that Ed came home on Tuesday and is with us this morning." There was a joyful clapping of hands! He came home to his church family and they received him. There had been repentance and forgiveness. Ed had met God's requirements and could once again enjoy fellowship with other believers.

At the end of the service, when the invitation was given for rededication of our lives to Christ, Ed and Jeanne walked the aisle as a testimony to God's grace. Ed was indicating to all of us that he wanted to serve the Lord the rest of his life.

My husband and I went up to stand beside them. What a joy it was to talk to them in the counseling room. Tears flowed freely as Ed thanked the Lord for his mercy, his love, and forgiveness.

It was then that I had suggested the lunch meeting at which Ed later told us how he was healed in prison.

"Yes, I would like that," he said. "I want to tell you what God has done in my life."

Postscript

Ed now witnesses to the grace and mercy of God in his life. His prison experience was not a waste. It strengthened his desire to serve the Lord.

". . . love covers a multitude of sins" (1 Peter 4:8). Human forgiveness brings glory to God and gives health to body, soul, and mind. An unforgiving spirit hurts the person who carries the grudge. It eats away like a cancer and robs us of peace.

It's not enough to say, "I have forgiven you," if we then refuse to have anything to do with that person. We have an obligation to encourage the sinner, for in that way we follow the Lord's example and also build up the body of Christ.

It takes just a step to become a believer in Jesus Christ, but it takes many more steps to grow in the Christian life. There are many stumblings along the way. Because all of us sin and need to be forgiven, we must use the truth of 1 John 1:9 often, if we are to keep short accounts with the Lord.

"How do we know Ed is truly repentant?" someone asked me.

"We are told to leave judgments to the Lord," I said. "We are told to forgive seventy times seven. No one must try to play the part of the Holy Spirit."

All of us have been forgiven many times. The Lord's Prayer asks God to forgive us *as* we forgive those who sin against us. Unless we learn to forgive, we become consumed with hatred. Jesus came to restore the joy of our salvation. Because believers, too, must be committed to restoration, we must help those who have been caught in sinfulness.

Paul and I were in Ed's home when he got a phone

call from one of the inmates who wanted spiritual help. Ed could indeed help—he's been there!

It's been over a year since Ed's incarceration. He is now working for a Christian organization. He deeply regrets his sin and straying from the Lord, but God is using him to be a witness for him. God did not forsake Ed in prison and he never will.

But when the chief priests and the teachers of the law saw the wonderful things he [Jesus] did and the children shouting in the temple area, "Hosanna to the Son of David," they were indignant.

"Do you hear what these children are saying?" they asked him.

"Yes," replied Jesus, "have you never read, 'From the lips of children and infants you have ordained praise'?"

[Matthew 21:15–16]

19

Witnessing Starts at Home

When Easter services were over, Emily had a big question for her parents: "Why did Jesus have to die?"

"He died for our sins," her mother, Sandy, answered. "We are all sinners, and Jesus was the only one who could pay the penalty for our sins. He was the perfect sacrifice."

"What's a sacrifice?" the little girl asked.

"In the Old Testament, before Jesus' time, an animal

was slain to take the place of the person who sinned. It had to be a spotless lamb, goat, or bull—an animal without defect. This offering was to cover the sin until Jesus came. Only Jesus could truly substitute for our sins, and he sacrificed his life for us."

"Why was Jesus the perfect sacrifice?" Emily persisted.

"Because, even though he was human, he never sinned. When Jesus died on the cross, God was giving his Son to pay the penalty for *our* sins."

"But if Jesus died, God did, too, because they're the same. Right?"

"God the *Son* died on the cross and then arose from the dead. God the *Father* is up in heaven. When we receive Jesus as our Savior, God accepts us because of what his Son did on the cross for us. That's what John 3:16 means. 'For God so loved the world that he gave his one and only Son, that whoever believes in him shall not perish but have eternal life.'"

Sandy was ready with those answers because Jesus Christ was a reality in her own life. She had known the time would come when her daughter would have some questions about the Lord.

When Sandy shared this story with me, her eyes sparkled. She knew that Emily had listened carefully and learned the wonderful truths about Jesus Christ. What greater joy can a mother or father receive than to give their children the answer to eternal life!

Our friend Dale came to me at church one Sunday and said, "I really feel all stressed out. Between my business, preparing to move, and the kids underfoot, I wonder if I'm going to make it. Please pray for me. I'm so impatient with the children, and I really don't want to be that kind of father."

"I know four children can be a trial at times," I said. "I had three, and now I look back and all I can think of was the fun we had together. You'll make it. We parents all survive."

Dale said, "Let me tell you what happened yesterday. Because I wanted the house to look presentable for prospective buyers, I've been painting and fixing up the place. I noticed that someone had written on the freshly painted wall. I was sure Debbie was the culprit. So I called her and asked whether she had written on the wall.

"'No, Daddy,' our six-year-old replied.

"'Yes, you did,' I said. Of course, she broke out in tears, and afterwards I felt badly because I was really hard on her. But I knew she was the one who did it. How would you have handled the situation, Nellie?"

"It's easy to say *now* what I would have done. Although I've made mistakes and certainly wasn't a perfect parent, I'm older now and have learned from experience. It takes a lot of wisdom to raise children. Dale, you want to be a godly role model, right?"

"I sure do."

"If you think Debbie is having a problem with lying, why don't you say, 'Do you know who wrote on the wall?' If she says, 'No, Daddy,' say, 'Let's ask God to show us who did. We need to take care of this situation.' Ask her to pray, too. If she's guilty, she'll probably cry. But you must be gentle with her so she feels safe in telling you the truth."

"That's a good idea," Dale said. "I'll try to remember that."

Dale shared our conversation with his wife, Suzi,

who called me a couple of days later and said, "I need to tell you what happened next. Debbie came downstairs with a cut on the sleeve of her T-shirt. She'd obviously used the scissors on it, but I asked, 'Debbie, how did your sleeve get cut?'

"'I don't know, Mommy.'

"'You have no idea who did it?'

"'No, Mommy,' she said very softly.

"Then I said, 'Let's pray and ask God to show us who did it. We can't have anyone cutting up your clothes. I'll pray and then you pray.' Debbie prayed and went on her way, apparently not bothered at all. After dinner that night she came to me and said, 'I need to tell you something, Mommy. It has to be a secret.'

"'Oh, you've got a secret to tell me? Great,' I said.

"'Mom, I know who cut my T-shirt.'

"'You do? Tell me about it.'

"Debbie hung her head and struggled to speak. '*I* did it, Mom.' She couldn't stand it. She had lied before, but this time she had asked God to point out the guilty one and the pressure was too much. I told her, 'I'm glad you told me the truth. That's what God wants you to do. It also shows that the Spirit of God is working in your life. That's what happens when you receive Jesus as your Savior. God's Spirit lives in you and helps you to do what's right. I think it's important that we tell Daddy about this.'

"'Oh, Mom, do I have to tell him?' Debbie pleaded.

"'I'll go with you. It will be okay.' We went upstairs and Debbie told her dad what she had done.

"Dale said, 'It was wrong of you to do that, Debbie, but I'm glad you came and told me. You must always tell the truth. Tell me, Debbie, why did you cut your T-shirt?'

"'I wanted to be like you, Daddy. When you go running in the morning you put your black T-shirt on, and it has no sleeves. I want to look like you.'"

Suzi told me that Dale's heart melted. He took his daughter in his arms and said, "I think we can fix that. Mommy will take you shopping tomorrow. Maybe she can find a T-shirt just like mine. But please don't use the scissors on your clothes. You ruin them and I work hard to buy them for you." Debbie said she was very sorry and promised not to do it again.

"Debbie and I went shopping," Suzi told me. "We found a black sleeveless T-shirt just like Dale's."

Both Suzi and Dale were excited to see the change in their little girl. They thanked God that night for the working of the Holy Spirit in Debbie's heart.

Postscript

Jesus said, "Let the little children come to me, and do not hinder them, for the kingdom of heaven belongs to such as these" (Matt. 19:14). What a privilege it is to train up a child in the nurture and admonition of the Lord!

Young mothers often come to me and say, "I don't get out of the house very often. How can I be a witness for the Lord? I go around with guilt because I know God wants me to share my faith."

What I tell them is that teaching their children about Jesus Christ *is* being a faithful witness. It is also the most important thing a Christian can do as far as their training is concerned. Living a life consistent with what we teach is of equal importance. God wants parents to "train a child in the way he should go" (Prov. 22:6a). That is God's will, and he is pleased when we heed his command.

*For all have sinned and fall short of the glory of
God, and are justified freely by his grace through
the redemption that came by Jesus Christ.*

[Romans 3:23–24]

*[Jesus said:] "I tell you the truth, no one can see
the kingdom of God unless he is born again."*

[John 3:3]

20

The Truth Will Out

Nellie, our women's society is having a
series of talks on the religions of the
world," Anne, my neighbor, phoned and said. "You're
a religious person. How about attending a session or
two? We meet on Tuesday mornings from nine to
eleven. Are you free next Tuesday, and would you like to
come?"

"It sounds interesting," I answered. "Excuse me while
I check my calendar. . . . Yes, I'll be able to attend."

I looked forward to the meeting. The little Community Church was only a few blocks away. I had heard it
was liberal in doctrine and felt this might be a chance to

find out for myself. I had attended a wedding there once, but that was the only connection I had with this church.

Anne introduced me to several of her friends. We chatted while sipping coffee before the meeting started. They were friendly and made me feel welcome.

"Today," the moderator said with enthusiasm, "we'll be studying about our own religion, Christianity. Cynthia Adams, our speaker, teaches in our children's department. We're looking forward to hearing what she has to say."

Cynthia was an articulate speaker who talked to us simply and to the point. I was delighted to hear her say, "Even though we can't all be missionaries, we can all share our faith. Because we're all born into the world as sinners, the Bible says that we must be born again."

At that point a woman raised her hand and said, "But we've never been taught that at *this* church. I'm not a sinner—and I don't agree with what you're saying."

"We are studying the religions of the world," Cynthia said patiently to the woman. "Today I'm speaking about the Christian faith. I'm telling you what the Bible says. That's my source of information and my authority."

Although Cynthia's remarks caused quite an uproar, she kept her composure and continued in a gracious manner.

After the meeting was over, I waited to talk to her. "Have you been born again?" I asked.

"Yes, I have," she answered.

"I'm a born-again Christian, too," I said.

Cynthia beamed. "I thought I was the only believer here. God must have sent you here today for my encouragement," she said. "Let's meet for lunch next week."

On the way home, my neighbor Anne asked me how I liked the meeting.

I told her I agreed with the speaker: "She was right on target. I'm sorry the woman in the audience gave her a hard time. Cynthia knew what she was talking about. The Bible was her reference book. What other source is there for truth?"

"Well, I guess we don't know much about that," Anne dismissed the matter.

I went to that church with Anne several times after that, but found it to be cold and lifeless. They did not seem to really welcome the gospel.

Anne's parents lived a few blocks away. When Anne's father died suddenly at home, her mother was devastated and inconsolable. Anne called me and said, "I don't know what to do about my mother. Will you come over and talk to her? Maybe you can help her."

When I went to the house, I found Anne's mother in bed. She was usually a very dignified woman, but today she was weeping uncontrollably and still in shock.

I sat down beside her bed, took her hand, and said, "I'm going to pray for you." She squeezed my hand tightly. While I prayed, she cried but still hung on to my hand. I stayed with her for several hours. Before I left, I shared the gospel with her and said, "God is your only source of help. When you feel better, perhaps we can talk again."

Later Anne and her family thanked me repeatedly for taking the time to talk and pray with her mother.

Several other neighbors have asked me to pray when an emergency arose in their families. "We know you get through to God," one woman said. But when things got better, most of them weren't interested in knowing more about God—which I find very sad.

When I met Cynthia for lunch, I asked her how she got involved in the church at which I had heard her speak.

"We moved to this area from the east side of the city and wanted to attend a church near our home. We thought the Community Church would be the answer. I now have my doubts, but I'll continue to teach my Sunday school class and see if I can be an influence in the children's lives."

"How did you become a Christian?" I asked.

"I accepted Christ when I was twelve years old, at a church on the other side of town. It took a long time before I grew spiritually, however. An interesting thing happened one day when I was on my way to work. On the bus I noticed the lady next to me reading some shorthand notes. I knew shorthand well, and my eyes caught the Scripture references she had written on a pad. I didn't say anything at first, but we both got off at the same stop. Since it was raining, she offered to share her umbrella.

"'I noticed you were reading Scripture,' I said to her.

"'Yes, I'm memorizing them for my class,' she told me. 'I attend a Bible class and we have a wonderful teacher.'

"When I told her I was a Christian and wanted to learn more about the Bible, she said I was welcome to come. That was God's provision for me," Cynthia said. "I had a hunger for the Word and I was satisfied. The teacher knew the Bible well and I ate it up, much like a starving child. That's how I began to grow as a Christian. Oh, the teacher's name was David Gillespie. Have you ever heard of him, Nellie?"

"Of course. He came to our church after he retired," I answered. "I loved hearing him speak from time to time. He's now with the Lord."

Cynthia and I had a good time getting better acquainted. When it was time to get back to our families, we promised to keep in touch. "Before we leave may I ask you to pray for my husband?" Cynthia asked me. "I'm concerned about him. Bob's a wonderful man, but he doesn't know the Lord."

We prayed together and I promised that Paul and I would continue to remember Bob in prayer.

It was a sad day when, sometime after that, Cynthia called and said, "I won't be teaching my Sunday school class any longer."

"What happened?" I wanted to know.

"One of the officers in the church stood outside my classroom and heard me talking about confessing our sins and our need to receive Christ as our Savior. He reported it to the elders and I was told I could not talk about sin to the children because 'We don't believe in teaching our children such things.'

"'Then I resign,' I told him. 'If I can't teach Bible truth, I don't belong here.' Then I went home and told Bob that we no longer were members of that church and would have to find another place to worship. Bob took it well. 'It's up to you to find another church,' he said."

"I'd love to have you come to our church," I said.

"Nellie, your church is so big, but I've heard about a small evangelical group I'd like to try. Perhaps Bob can get acquainted with some of the men. It would help him to know some real Christians on a personal basis."

Paul and I continued to pray for Bob. One day Cynthia called and said, "Bob came to Christ last night. It's wonderful! He already wants to get busy for the Lord. He has seen such a difference in the two churches. God has opened his heart and his eyes. I'm so happy and grateful to the Lord."

Cynthia and I continued to see and encourage each other. One day she said, "I love our little fellowship group, but there's nothing for my son. There are no boys his age. We've decided to come to your church so he can get into a young people's group." Of course I was delighted.

Even though we now attend the same church, we rarely get together. Cynthia and Bob are busy people, and I spend a lot of my time speaking and writing. But when Cynthia and I do see each other, we are reminded of how God brought us together—and we are thankful.

Postscript

It is dangerous to attend a church where the Bible is not honored as the authoritative Word of God. Such a church is preaching "a different gospel" (Gal. 1:6). Many churches do not want to talk about sin. It makes them feel uncomfortable, so they pretend there is no such thing. When my rabbi friend said to me, "We don't talk about sin—only 'missing the mark'"—I realized that "missing the mark" feels more comfortable. People say, "We all make mistakes," as if to excuse their wrongdoing. For many Christians, church has become nothing more than a social gathering place.

How blessed we are when we confess our sins and experience God's cleansing and forgiveness. Then we are free of sin's burden—free to do what is right.

One day, when we see Christ, we will be without sin. Until then, when we do become aware that we have sinned we can and must confess it.

> If we claim to be without sin, we deceive ourselves and the truth is not in us. If we confess our sins, he is faithful and just and will forgive us our sins and purify us from all unrighteousness. If we claim we have not sinned, we make him out to be a liar and his word has no place in our lives.
>
> [1 John 1:8–10]

Whether you turn to the right or to the left, your ears will hear a voice behind you, saying, "This is the way; walk in it."

[Isaiah 30:21]

21

The Ear Specialist Listens

My friend Libby came to me one day and said excitedly, "Have I got a story for you! I can hardly wait to tell you."

"Let's have lunch together. I'd like to hear it," I said.

We both had busy schedules for the next few weeks, but we finally got together in a local restaurant. While waiting to be served, I told Libby I had been looking forward to hearing her story and asked what had happened to get her so excited.

"I've been having inner-ear problems," Libby said. "The doctor told me I needed to have a balance function test and said it would only take about an hour. When I arrived at the hospital for the test, they put me in a tiny room—I felt like I was in a telephone booth. I was told to lie down on a table and look up at the lights in the ceiling. Doctor Abraham noticed I was a bit nervous so he asked whether I ever have problems with claustrophobia.

"'Sometimes,' I told him, 'but I think I'll be all right.'

"The doctor then said, 'I'm going to fill your ears with water. First cold, then hot. This part of the test will take about twelve minutes. While this is going on, you must talk. Say anything you want, but you must keep talking.' Dr. Abraham sat outside the booth with earphones on, ready to record what he heard. I wasn't prepared, so I didn't know what to say. I started out by talking in general about my family, children, and grandchildren. I also mentioned that my husband was the business administrator at our church.

"When the test was over I felt nauseous, so the doctor had me lie quiet for a while. As I was lying on the table I thought, *I really blew it. It's not very often that I am asked to say anything I want and have a captive audience. I should have given my testimony. If I ever get a chance like this again, I won't muff it.*

"When Doctor Abraham returned, I said, 'I feel much better now.' He told me to go and get a sandwich. Then they would have to take another test. Even though the first test made me feel ill, I was glad that God was giving me a second chance to be a good witness. How many times does a person get an opportunity to talk about the Lord to a captive audience!

"When I returned to the examining room, the doctor said, 'This time the test will only take five minutes. But you mustn't stop talking.' This is what I said, Nellie:

My grandmother was a great influence in my life. She was a no-nonsense woman but was full of love and compassion. She wouldn't let us get away with a thing and taught us about God's standards.

When I was old enough to understand the gospel, I had no problem accepting it. When my Sunday school teacher asked me if I would like to receive Jesus Christ as my Savior, it was as though I had been waiting for this moment. Because I realized he paid the penalty for my sin and took all of my guilt, I now wanted to live to honor the Lord.

We raised our children to understand that although God loved them, they had to have a personal relationship with him. They could have that by recognizing that they were sinners and asking Jesus Christ to be their Savior. We also impressed them with the facts that lying and being mean and selfish were sinful.

I'm happy to say that all of our children accepted Jesus Christ. We continued to teach them biblical principles about church attendance, not only on Sunday but at Wednesday evening prayer meetings. We also taught them the importance of tithing.

Now we are happy to see our grandchildren attend a Christian school. They have had the same Christian influence as our children, their parents. We have much for which to be thankful. . . .

"At that point the doctor said, 'That's enough. I'll now take the tests to be evaluated.'

"Before Doctor Abraham left, he said, 'It's amazing what people say in a booth. Sometimes I feel that most people have nothing to say—no experience worth repeating. But what *you* were saying was so interesting I almost forgot to work the computer. I had a feeling you could have talked on about your life for a couple of days. But tell me, why does your church need a business manager?'

"I explained that a church has the responsibility for

the offerings and tithes of the congregation, that it must pay salaries to our missionaries and staff as well as handle expenses for heating and lighting of our building. I told him that businessmen who are members of our church are chosen to determine how the money should be spent.

"He also asked about our school. When I told him that we consider our school a mission field, I added, 'We are unhappy about what our children learn in public school.'

"Finally the doctor said, 'I'm impressed with what you've said. I'd like my children to have what yours had. Would it be all right if we visit your church?'

"'By all means,' I told him. And I'm certainly looking forward to seeing him in church and introducing him to our friends."

Postscript

I'm glad Libby shared that experience with me. Her unique opportunity to witness is but one more example that such moments stand before us every day, begging to be used as testimony for the Lord.

The seed has been sown. Who will come along to water it? If the doctor and his family do come to our church, they will be drenched with the water of the Word and be surrounded by the sunshine of God's love. All believers must be a part of that process.

It is God's will that "at the name of Jesus every knee should bow, in heaven and on earth and under the earth, and every tongue confess that Jesus Christ is Lord, to the glory of God the Father" (Phil. 2:10–11).

Be wise in the way you act toward outsiders; make the most of every opportunity. Let your conversation be always full of grace, seasoned with salt, so that you may know how to answer everyone.

[Colossians 4:5–6]

22

Opportunity Knocks

"If you care to wait, your car will be ready in about a half an hour," the mechanic said.

"How nice," I responded. "I came prepared for a much longer stay."

I had brought along a copy of *What Would You Have Said?* and sat down on a nearby bench to relax and reread some portions of it.

No sooner had I started to read when another customer approached me and said, "Do you mind if I sit next to you? This is the only available bench."

"No, I don't mind." I moved over to give the man more space and continued with my reading.

"Is that a good book?" he asked.

"Well—I wrote it. You be the judge."

"May I see it?" he asked.

I gave him the book, and he began to read the dedication and the foreword. "This is great. I've never met a real live author before. Wow!"

"It's no big deal," I said. "I'm writing for the one who guides me and impresses me with the truth."

"Who's that?" the man asked.

"Jesus Christ," I answered. Then I asked, "Do you pray?"

"I pray every day," he said. "I pray in my own way, however."

"If you pray to God the Father, you have to pray according to his rules," I commented.

"What are his rules?"

"The Bible says that Jesus Christ is the only mediator we need. God is holy and man is sinful, so we can't just rush into his presence. We have to come in the name of Jesus. He died for our sins and is the only sinless one. That's the reason we always end our prayers with the words 'in Jesus' name.'"

I reached in my purse and gave him my witnessing tool, *The Four Spiritual Laws.* I explained that the booklet would give him the basics of what salvation is all about.

He opened it and started to read. "Look at this," he said in amazement. "I'm a sinner, just like it says. My wife believes this stuff. She's been wanting me to go to church with her for a long time. Maybe I ought to look into it."

The attendant came and said, "Mrs. Pickard, your car is ready."

"I have to leave now," I said to the man. "But reading this will show you the remedy for your sin. Keep reading the booklet. All the verses in it are from the Bible, which makes what it says authentic. I also suggest you attend church with your wife. It sounds to me like she's on the right track."

"Thanks," he said. "I appreciate your talking to me. I'll show this booklet to my wife. She'll be glad to hear that someone influenced me to go to church."

"A wife's prayer goes a long way," I said with a smile and left.

As I have said many times before, God puts opportunities all around us. Our job is to throw out the bait and see if we can get a nibble on the line.

I rarely leave the house without discovering an opportunity to say something about God, Jesus Christ, or the Bible. I don't believe in "collar grabbing." I don't need to do that, and I don't believe God wants believers to back people into a corner. But when my spiritual antenna goes up, I'm not timid either (although I once was). Because God arranges the appointments, I have many delightful experiences when I least expect them.

The other day I had a problem at the market. I couldn't find fish sticks in the frozen-food section and had asked the young man working nearby where they were.

"They're at the other end of this aisle," he had said, but I looked at all the items in the freezer and still couldn't find them.

The young man saw my dilemma and approached me. "*Now* what are you looking for?" he asked with a grin on his face.

"I'm embarrassed, but I haven't found the fish sticks yet."

"Oh, they're in the next aisle. Right around the corner."

"I'm sorry," I said. "I guess I didn't listen very well."

"Don't blame yourself. I didn't communicate properly," the clerk answered.

"I have the same problem at times," I said. "But there is one thing I *do* communicate well—the gospel of Jesus Christ."

Because the young man looked like he had gone into shock, I asked him, "Do you know what I mean by the gospel?"

"Yes, but no one has ever witnessed to me like that before. Do I know what the gospel is? You bet I do! The Lord got a hold of me three years ago. All I ever did was drink, party, and smoke pot. But let me tell you, my life has changed. It's completely turned around. I've never known such joy and peace. Life is worth living now. I drank to drown my thoughts. I didn't like myself. Now I work with people who have the same problem I had. I know where they're at and can show them a better life. By the way, do you know a lady by the name of Dorothy Lehman?" he asked.

"I sure do," I answered. "She sang at my daughter Karen's wedding."

"Well, she comes in the store and we talk. She's like a breath of fresh air."

"I'm glad you've met her," I said. "Dorothy is a wonderful Christian and one of the kindest people I know.

"What's your name?" I asked.

"David. Do you know, I believe God sent you in the store today—just to encourage me. I feel just great."

"I certainly agree that God does things like that. I feel great, too."

As I was about to leave, David said, "I hope you'll come in the store again and give me some tips on witnessing."

"I'll do better than that," I told him. "I'll give you a book I've written on witnessing."

I went to the car to get a copy of *What Do You Say When?* David met me in front of the store and said, "Let me tell you what I'll do. I'll read it and then pass it on to some of the employees. Maybe that will stimulate a discussion. I've already talked to some of them about the Lord."

I'm looking forward to seeing David again.

It's surprising how a conversation gets started. I don't plan these encounters. They just seem to happen, at least that's the way it appears to me. But I know God arranges them—like the time I went to a local discount store. I was in a hurry because I had shopped most of the afternoon and it was getting close to supper time. I knew I was taking advantage of my husband's good nature. *Just one more stop,* I thought. *It will only take a minute to buy the hose I so badly need.*

The checkout line presented a problem. I stood rather impatiently in a long line, waiting my turn. But I should have remembered that it's at times like this that God nudges me and gives me an exciting adventure in his service.

The woman in front of me turned and asked, "What do you do with a boy like mine? He won't say 'please.'"

Then she realized I didn't know what she was talking about and said, "We're visiting from Toronto. My son wanted a certain brand of jeans, and we thought this store would have them. He found the jeans and he wants them, but he won't say 'please.' What shall I do?"

I laughed, then turned to the young man and asked, "How old are you?"

With a smirk on his face he said, "Fourteen. And I don't know why I should have to say 'please.'"

"You are a very handsome young man—on the outside. I think you have some problems on the inside, however. Your mom is willing to buy you some new jeans, but your pride won't allow you to say 'please.' The Bible says that God hates pride. It is among the worst of sins. And do you know what? You are the loser, not your mom."

"He just won't get the jeans unless he can say 'please,'" his mother insisted. "I know what will happen. As soon as we get back to Toronto, he'll tell me he just has to have a new pair. I'll remind him of this incident, and he still won't get the jeans until he can learn to say 'please.'"

"If pride is a sin," the mother asked, "what is its counterpart?"

"Humility," I said.

"If we're humble, that pleases God, right?"

"Yes—and that's what Jesus said: 'For everyone who exalts himself will be humbled, and he who humbles himself will be exalted.' Those words are in Luke 14:11."

"I'm Jewish," the woman said. "But I like that." She held out her hand and thanked me for supporting her. But they left without the young man's new jeans!

When I got home and told Paul about the incident, he didn't mind having a late supper at all.

Postscript

I'm glad I told the Lord, "I want to be available to you for witnessing." Although I don't have to go looking for people, I do have to be alert. I now go shopping with a feeling of expectation, for I never know what God has lined up for me. Opportunities are everywhere.

Opportunity knocked when the man at the auto shop asked about my book. He couldn't have asked a better question. My mind went immediately to the subject I had written about. I love talking to people about the Lord and am always prepared. I'm glad he has a praying wife, but it's nice to be a part of influencing people for Jesus Christ.

Opportunity knocked when I met David in the freezer section of the grocery store. And it has opened up other opportunities to say a word for the Lord. I met the manager of the store the other day and told him that I had had a good conversation with his "prize worker."

"And who is that?" the manager asked with a grin.

"David," I said.

"He's a good kid," he commented. "But you should have known him before. He was into all sorts of things. He's a different person now."

"I know. He told me that Jesus Christ has made the difference in his life. He also mentioned that your wife is ill. He's praying for her and so am I."

The manager was visibly moved and said, "I really appreciate that. She needs all the prayers she can get. She's had cancer, but I believe she's going to be all right."

"It's amazing what God can do, isn't it?" I said.

"It sure is." He gave me a big smile.

Opportunity knocked again at the discount store. The woman in line was frustrated with her son's prideful obstinance and turned to me for support. My mind immediately went to my source of help: God's Word. A tiny mustard seed has been planted. Only the Spirit of God can germinate it.

In ourselves we are weak and timid, but when the Holy Spirit is in us, we have the power to witness. He does the work through us. We are God's tools and he uses us as he sees fit. He just wants us to be ready and willing when opportunity knocks.

If we claim to be without sin, we deceive our-
selves and the truth is not in us. If we confess our
sins, he is faithful and just and will forgive us our
sins and purify us from all unrighteousness. If we
claim we have not sinned, we make him out to be
a liar and his word has no place in our lives.

[1 John 1:8–10]

23

Blessed Assurance

My friend Casey asked me to comment on people who believe they can be saved but worry that if they sin they are lost again. "I visit a man in a nursing home who has no peace," he said. "He says he's never sure from one day to the next if he's really saved. Nellie, have you had any experience with people who are insecure about their salvation?"

"Yes, I have," I said. "And it's certainly important for a believer's peace of mind to feel secure in Christ."

Then I told Casey about my favorite aunt, who—like the man in the nursing home—once believed that even

after accepting Christ as Savior, salvation could be lost
if a person sinned.

For quite some time, my aunt had been in a contin-
uous state of misery because she didn't know for sure if
she was going to heaven when she died. We had many
discussions about it. I loved my aunt, but it grieved me
to see her in such a state. I had to be careful and
wanted to be respectful. I'm sorry to say, I did argue
with her once in a while, but she was a sweet person
and never got angry.

What this situation did for me was cause me to
search the Scriptures for answers. I was rather young at
the time, so I'm afraid that even though I wanted to
help my aunt, I also wanted to prove to her that I was
right. That was pride on my part, and God calls that
sin. Yes, I sinned by my attitude, but God didn't erase
my name from the Book of Life. Instead he gently
taught me the better way.

My aunt later moved to California and I didn't see
her for many years. When she came back for a visit we
had a long talk. The first thing I said to her was, "Aun-
tie, I want to apologize to you for trying to prove you
wrong about the security of the believer. I really didn't
have a right attitude."

"I don't remember that at all," she said. "But I now
know that when I die I'm going to be with the Lord. I
am sure of that. I've been attending 'Bible Study Fellowship' in California. We compare Scripture with
Scripture to find the answer for our hope. I now understand what it means to have eternal life. Jesus paid for
my salvation, and I'm truly secure in him. He went to
prepare a place for me. I'm no longer worried about
my future. I believe—just like you." She beamed and
gave me a hug.

She was a different person after that. I could see that she had real peace. My aunt has since passed away, and I know she's with the Lord.

I have found some verses that are helpful to Christians who, like my aunt, are not sure about their salvation. John 10:27–30 is a beautiful passage to read and remember. Jesus said:

> "My sheep listen to my voice; I know them, and they follow me. I give them eternal life, and they shall never perish; no one can snatch them out of my hand. My Father, who has given them to me, is greater than all; no one can snatch them out of my Father's hand. I and the Father are one."

Jesus is the Good Shepherd. He is in control. I believe a person who *claims* to have accepted Christ, yet continually lives in a state of sin, thereby rebelling against God, probably isn't saved. The difference between a truly born-again believer and an unbeliever is that the believer runs away from sin and the unbeliever runs *after* it. When the believer does fall into sin and the Spirit of God convicts him, God has made a provision for that: "If we confess our sins, he is faithful and just and will forgive us our sins and purify us from all unrighteousness" (1 John 1:9).

That was written to Christians. None of us is perfect, but our goal is to fulfill God's requirements. We press on toward that goal, as Paul says in Philippians 3:14. We don't give up, because we know we are God's children and must take one step after another, growing in knowledge of his will and his loving grace. He is perfect and we are not, but we come to God through the perfection of our Savior. He is our righteousness, and God the Father looks at us through Jesus Christ to see if we are covered by his blood.

Hebrews 12 says this so well that we should read the entire chapter often and especially keep verses 6 through 8 in our hearts:

> In your struggle against sin, you have not yet resisted to the point of shedding blood. And you have forgotten that word of encouragement that addresses you as sons:
>
> "My son, do not make light of the Lord's discipline;
>   and do not lose heart when he rebukes you,
> because the Lord disciplines those he loves,
>   and he punishes everyone he accepts as a son."
>
> Endure hardship as discipline; God is treating you as sons. For what son is not disciplined by his father? If you are not disciplined (and everyone undergoes discipline), then you are illegitimate children and not true sons.

A person may be confused as to whether or not he or she is saved or lost. If that is the case, it is best to check to see if that person is truly born again. Ask, "Have you received Jesus Christ as your sacrifice for sin? Have you told him you want to live for him and have him guide and direct your life?" If the answer is "yes," you might double-check by asking, "Do you have a desire to read the Bible and obey his commands?" If the answer again is "yes," it is a good indication that this person is in the family of God.

Postscript

The apostle John said: "My dear children, I write this to you so that you will not sin. But if anybody does sin, we have one who speaks to the Father in our defense—Jesus Christ, the Righteous One. He is the atoning sacrifice for our sins, and not only for ours but also for the sins of the whole world" (1 John 2:1–2).

All of us as believers must accept the fact that we will not be perfect until we are with our perfect Redeemer in heaven. Until then, we need to keep growing in Christ and press on toward that goal.

May you enjoy the abundant life that Christ came to give all who confess their sinfulness, accept him as Savior, and dedicate their lives to serving the Lord.